M000276663

What Readers Are Saying About
The ThoughtWorks Anthology 2

ThoughtWorks is a company I've long admired from afar. So when a request to review *The ThoughtWorks Anthology 2* came up, I gladly accepted. I particularly like the fact that ThoughtWorkers have practical field experience, and their articles reflect it. The skills of the respective writers really show through in the content.

More importantly, these topics have direct relevance to our daily work as software developers. We may very well find ourselves taking on the advice promoted by these authors on our next task or project.

Grab a copy; I'm confident that you'll be glad you did.

➤ **Eitan Suez**
   Independent consultant, speaker

What's nice about *The ThoughtWorks Anthology 2* is the breadth of topics covered. Technology has been changing rapidly, which has had a strong impact on developers. I like that the anthology covers changes about languages, integration, and testing as well as how Java development on the server side has changed. The anthology will be useful for both new developers and seasoned developers transitioning to the newer development landscapes.

➤ **Greg Ostravich**
   IT professional, CDOT

The latest anthology from ThoughtWorks brings together the latest trends in languages, testing, and continuous delivery but keeps a highly practical focus. Once again, ThoughtWorks has pulled together a range of timely, relevant, practical, and engaging articles designed to help software developers enhance their craft.

It's a must-read for any professional software developer.

➤ **Peter Bell**
  Senior VP engineering and senior fellow, General Assembly

The ThoughtWorks Anthology 2

More Essays on Software Technology and Innovation

Farooq Ali

Brian Blignaut

Neal Ford

Luca Grulla

Aman King

Marc McNeill

Mark Needham

Rebecca Parsons

Ola Bini

James Bull

Martin Fowler

Alistair Jones

Patrick Kua

Julio Maia

Sam Newman

Cosmin Stejerean

The Pragmatic Bookshelf

Dallas, Texas • Raleigh, North Carolina

Many of the designations used by manufacturers and sellers to distinguish their products are claimed as trademarks. Where those designations appear in this book, and The Pragmatic Programmers, LLC was aware of a trademark claim, the designations have been printed in initial capital letters or in all capitals. The Pragmatic Starter Kit, The Pragmatic Programmer, Pragmatic Programming, Pragmatic Bookshelf, PragProg and the linking *g* device are trademarks of The Pragmatic Programmers, LLC.

Every precaution was taken in the preparation of this book. However, the publisher assumes no responsibility for errors or omissions, or for damages that may result from the use of information (including program listings) contained herein.

Our Pragmatic courses, workshops, and other products can help you and your team create better software and have more fun. For more information, as well as the latest Pragmatic titles, please visit us at *http://pragprog.com*.

The team that produced this book includes:

Michael Swaine (editor)
Potomac Indexing, LLC (indexer)
Kim Wimpsett (copyeditor)
David J Kelly (typesetter)
Janet Furlow (producer)
Juliet Benda (rights)
Ellie Callahan (support)

Copyright © 2012 ThoughtWorks.
All rights reserved.

No part of this publication may be reproduced, stored in a retrieval system, or transmitted, in any form, or by any means, electronic, mechanical, photocopying, recording, or otherwise, without the prior consent of the publisher.

Printed in the United States of America.
ISBN-13: 978-1-937785-00-0
Printed on acid-free paper.
Book version: P1.0—October 2012

Contents

Part II — Testing

Part III — Issues in Software Development

Part IV — Data Visualization

Preface

by Rebecca Parsons and Martin Fowler

While many companies are primarily defined by a business model, Thought-Works is primarily defined by a social model. We define three pillars to measure success in our business and to influence our business decisions.

- Run a sustainable business.

- Champion software excellence, and revolutionize IT.

- Advocate passionately for social and economic justice.

This ThoughtWorks business and social model continues to motivate us to challenge notions about organizational structure and business success. This social experiment that is ThoughtWorks will of course evolve, but we'd like to think ThoughtWorks will still be around and shaking things up in 100 years. And if you're around then, think of what a shelf of anthologies you'll have to leaf through!

Rebecca Parsons
rjparson@thoughtworks.com
June 2012

Martin Fowler
fowler@acm.org
June 2012

About the Authors

Farooq Ali

As a specialized-generalist, T-shaped thinker, Farooq loves to help teams create innovative solutions by looking at problems from many different angles. As a lead consultant, he's worn many different hats over the years at ThoughtWorks: developer, business analyst, project manager, experience designer. Farooq has always had a strong passion for visual thinking, be it in product ideation, code aesthetics, or data analysis. These days he heads the ThoughtWorks Social Impact Program in the Americas, helping tackle problems that lie at the intersection of technology, innovation, and social impact.

Ola Bini

Ola Bini works as a language geek for ThoughtWorks in Chicago. He is from Sweden, but don't hold that against him. He is one of the JRuby core developers and has been involved in JRuby development since 2006. At one point in time, Ola got tired of all existing programming languages and decided to create his own, called Ioke. Then he did it again and started work on Seph. He wrote a book called *Practical JRuby* on Rails projects for Apress, coauthered *Using JRuby* for the Pragmatic Programmers, talked at numerous conferences, and contributed to a large number of open source projects. He is also a member of the JSR292 Expert Group.

His main passion lies in implementing languages, working on regular expression engines, and trying to figure out how to create good YAML parsers.

Brian Blignaut

Brian worked at ThoughtWorks as a lead consultant for more than three years. During that time he worked on the delivery of a number of bespoke software systems for high-profile clients, from large customer-facing websites to real-time stream computing platforms. He has done a number of talks on

JavaScript testing and currently works as an independent software consultant in London.

James Bull

James is an agile software developer with a background in QA. He has been involved in many test automation efforts with ThoughtWorks and strongly believes that a good test suite is a test suite the whole team shares. When he's not fiddling around with computers, he's fiddling around with cars.

Neal Ford

Neal Ford is director, software architect, and meme wrangler at ThoughtWorks. He is also the designer and developer of applications, magazine articles, video/DVD presentations, and author/editor/contributor for eight books spanning a variety of subjects and technologies. He focuses on designing and building large-scale enterprise applications. He is also an internationally acclaimed speaker, speaking at more than 300 developer conferences world-wide and delivering more than 2,000 presentations.

Check out his website at http://nealford.com. He welcomes feedback and can be reached at nford@thoughtworks.com.

Martin Fowler

Martin is a self-described author, speaker...essentially a loud-mouthed pundit on the topic of software development. He has worked in the software industry since the mid-1980s where he got into the then-new world of object-oriented software. He spent much of the 1990s as a consultant and trainer, helping people develop object-oriented systems, with a focus on enterprise applications. In 2000 he joined ThoughtWorks.

His main interest is to understand how to design software systems so as to maximize the productivity of development teams. In doing this, he strives to understand the patterns of good software design and also the processes that support software design. Martin has become a big fan of Agile approaches and the resulting focus on evolutionary software design.

Luca Grulla

After four years in ThoughtWorks as a lead consultant helping clients in adopting Agile and Lean practices and in delivering quality software, Luca now works as a senior developer at Forward in London. In his current role, he engages in experimenting with languages and technologies while pushing new features in production several times a day. He is also an active member of the global IT community, being a regular speaker to international events and taking part as a program committee member to the organization of several European conferences (Italian Agile Day, EuroClojure).

Alistair Jones

Alistair Jones plays the roles of developer, technical lead, architect, and coach. He builds teams that make good technical decisions and produce great software. He likes to demonstrate that Agile methods both require and enable greater discipline than older ways of delivering software.

Aman King

Aman King is an application developer. He has worked on complex business applications as part of distributed Agile teams. He lives and breathes TDD and is known to refactor with a vengeance!

Patrick Kua

Patrick Kua works as an active, generalizing specialist for ThoughtWorks and dislikes being put into a box. Patrick is often found leading technical teams, frequently coaching people and organizations in Lean and Agile methods, and sometimes facilitating situations beyond adversity. Patrick is fascinated by elements of learning and continuous improvement, always helping others to develop enthusiasm for these same elements.

Marc McNeill

Marc is passionate about bringing multidisciplinary teams together to build great customer experiences. With a PhD in human factors, he spent seven years at ThoughtWorks and introduced design thinking and Lean start-up ideas into client projects across the world. With his fast pace and visual focus, he helped teams take nascent ideas and turn them into successful products through rapid and continual "test and learn" cycles. He is the author of the book *Agile Experience Design* (with Lindsay Ratcliffe) and is @dancingmango.

Julio Maia

Julio Maia has been working for the last five years as a technical consultant at ThoughtWorks. He has been helping clients to build software solutions by dealing with problems related to integration, automation, operations, testing infrastructure, and application development.

Mark Needham

Mark Needham is a software developer at ThoughtWorks and has worked there for the past six years using Agile methods to help clients solve problems using C#, Java, Ruby, and Scala.

Sam Newman

Sam Newman has been a technical consultant at ThoughtWorks for more than eight years. He has worked in a variety of companies and is still passionate about the role that emerging technologies can have in broadening the impact of IT.

Rebecca Parsons

Rebecca Parsons currently serves as ThoughtWorks' chief technology officer and has been involved in technology far longer than she cares to contemplate. She is passionate about programming languages specifically and technology in general. She received her PhD in computer science from Rice University, focusing in programming language semantics and compilers. She has also done work in evolutionary computation and computational biology.

Cosmin Stejerean

Cosmin Stejerean has been creating software professionally for more than eight years. He works as an operations engineer at Simple and lives in Dallas, Texas. Previously he traveled around the world as a lead consultant and trainer at ThoughtWorks.

CHAPTER 1

Introduction

by Neal Ford

I love anthologies. When I was a lad, I was a huge fan of science fiction. I was lucky to have access to a rich ecosystem of sci-fi magazines. Every year, each magazine would take its very best stories and anthologize them, presenting the cream of the crop.

I whiled away many hours reading those best-of collections. I loved those anthologies because each story had a different author; the change in style was refreshing as I moved from story to story. I loved the fact that each story has its own universe, with its own assumptions and context.

In later years, I edited and contributed to several (nonfiction) anthologies, including the first *The ThoughtWorks Anthology [Inc08]*. In the rapidly changing world of software, anthologies fill an important temporal niche, between blogs and magazines at one end and single-topic books at the other. Anthologies like this one represent a snapshot in time. With multiple authors and themes, they can cover process, technology, philosophy, and many more ideas currently at the forefront.

This is the second *The ThoughtWorks Anthology [Inc08]*. For the first one, Rebecca Parsons sent out a call for papers and received enough quality submissions to produce an excellent and broad-ranging anthology. When it came time to create a second edition, we sent out a similar call. However, in the interim, everyone had heard about the first anthology, so interest was much higher for the second round. We received more than 100 abstracts, many of them stunningly good. Because of the overwhelming response, we pulled in the ThoughtWorks Technology Advisory Board, an internal body that assists the CTO, to help filter and evaluate the abstracts. The board members winnowed the submissions to this select group. This edition of *The ThoughtWorks Anthology [Inc08]* represents the best of the best.

As Rebecca's preface to this edition shows, ThoughtWorks is a company that values diversity, and that includes diversity of thought. Some of the most enjoyable things we do at ThoughtWorks are to hang out after hours to see what odd hobbies are being indulged and participate in lunchtime conversations that range far and wide, frequently far beyond software. You get a feel for that diversity, I think, in these essays. While they all pertain to software development, they are otherwise quite individual.

This diversity allows you to browse the book in several ways.

If, like me, you enjoy the jolt of shifting contexts that different authors bring, you can safely read this book front to back. But you can also consume it along several broad themes.

If you are an Agile software process fan, check out Chapter 11, *Driving Innovation into Delivery*, on page 179. This chapter discusses techniques to inject innovation into your delivery pipeline, or you could start with Chapter 9, *Taming the Integration Problem*, on page 161, which covers sophisticated techniques for the sticky problem of integrating disparate systems.

If, on the other hand, you want to step down the spectrum toward the intersection of Agile and technical topics, check out Chapter 7, *Building Better Acceptance Tests*, on page 123; Chapter 5, *Extreme Performance Testing*, on page 89; and Chapter 6, *Take Your JavaScript for a Test-Drive*, on page 109—all of which cover aspects of testing in projects.

Leaning further toward purely technical topics, we have Chapter 10, *Feature Toggles in Practice*, on page 169; Chapter 4, *Functional Programming Techniques in Object-Oriented Languages*, on page 71; Chapter 8, *Modern Java Web Applications*, on page 143; Chapter 3, *Object-Oriented Programming: Objects over Classes*, on page 41; and Chapter 2, *The Most Interesting Languages*, on page 5.

Finally, if you believe the adage about pictures and words, Chapter 12, *A Thousand Words*, on page 197 shows how to create compelling visualizations from technical artifacts.

Of course, there is no wrong order to read this book. All of the authors composed these essays in their own nonexistent "spare" time, forsaking (for the duration) family, friends, and fun. That passion and dedication for conveying information comes across in the essays. We hope you enjoy reading them as much as we enjoyed writing them.

Part I

Languages

Three ThoughtWorkers explore programming languages with essays on object-oriented programming, functional programming, and a survey of some of the currently most interesting languages.

CHAPTER 2

The Most Interesting Languages

by Ola Bini

The Tao of Programming

The Tao gave birth to machine language. Machine language gave birth to the assembler.

The assembler gave birth to the compiler. Now there are 10,000 languages.

Each language has its purpose, however humble. Each language expresses the yin and yang of software. Each language has its place within the Tao.

But do not program in COBOL if you can avoid it.

A language renaissance is brewing. It has been going on for a few years, and the times we are living through right now might very well be the most interesting for language geeks since the 1970s. We are seeing many new languages being created, but we are also seeing a resurgence of older languages that are now finding a new niche—or as with Erlang, the problem it is solving has suddenly become crucial.

Why are we seeing such a renaissance right now? A big part of it is that we are trying to solve harder problems. We are working with larger and larger code bases, and we are finding that the traditional approaches just don't work anymore. We are working under larger and larger time pressures—especially start-ups that live and die by how fast they can get their products out. And we are solving problems that require concurrency and parallel execution to work well. Our traditional approaches have been woefully inadequate for these problems, so many developers are turning to different languages in the hope that it will become easier to solve their problem in that language.

At the same time that the need for new approaches grows greater, we also have extremely powerful resources at our disposal to create languages. The tools necessary to create a language are now at the level where you can cobble together a working language in just a few days. And once you have a running language, you can put it on any of the available mature platforms (like the JVM, the CLR, or LLVM). Once your language runs on any of these platforms, you get access to all the libraries, frameworks, and tools that make these platforms so powerful, which means the language creator doesn't have to reinvent the wheel.

This essay is about some interesting languages right now. I wanted to enumerate a few of the languages I think would give any programmer the most out of learning them. Any such list is prone to subjectivity and time sensitivity. My hope is that this list of languages is robust enough to still be true in a few years.

2.1   Why Languages Matter

One of the fundamental results of computer science is the Church-Turing thesis. It and related results effectively mean that at a fundamental level, there is no difference between languages. What you can do with one language, you can do with any other.

So, why do we care about differences among programming languages? Why shouldn't you just continue writing everything you write in Java? Come to think of it, why did anyone invent Java—and why did anyone start using it if it doesn't matter? Joking aside, there is a significant point here. We care about programming languages for the simple reason that different languages are better at different things. Even though you can do anything in any language, in many cases the best way of doing something in one language is to create an interpreter for a different language. This is sometimes referred to as Greenspun's Tenth Rule of Programming, which goes like this:

> Any sufficiently complicated C or Fortran program contains an ad hoc, informally specified, bug-ridden, slow implementation of half of Common Lisp.

It turns out that most languages can do most things, but the difference is in how easy or hard it is to achieve something. So, choosing the right language for a task means you are making everything else easier for you down the line. Knowing more than one language means you have more options for solving a specific problem.

In my opinion, the language you use is your most important choice as a programmer. Everything else depends on the language, so you should take care when choosing what language to use. Your project will live and die by this choice.

2.2 A Few Languages

I know I can't make everyone happy in an essay like this. If you don't see your favorite language on this list, that doesn't mean I find it uninteresting. I considered a large number of languages for this list but in the end couldn't make a place for all of them—so I chose the ones I find have the most to give in different categories. Anyone else making a list like this would definitely come up with a different one. So if you are disappointed in not seeing your favorite language on this list, write me and tell me why your language should be here. Or even better, write a blog post following the same pattern, introducing your favorite interesting language.

This essay won't contain instructions on how to find or install the introduced languages. Instructions like those have a tendency to quickly become outdated, so I recommend everyone use Google instead. Neither will I guide you through every aspect of the languages shown. Instead, I want to show a glimpse of how the language works and try to whet your appetite.

Clojure

Rich Hickey released the first version of Clojure in 2007. Since then, Clojure's popularity has grown rapidly, and it has now commercial backing, a large amount of donated development funds, and several very good books about it. The language is also moving very quickly—since the first release, there have been four major releases: 1.0, 1.1, 1.2, and 1.3. All of these have added and improved substantially on the language.

Clojure is a Lisp. However, it is neither a Common Lisp nor a Scheme implementation. Instead, it's a new version of a Lisp with inspiration taken from several different languages. It runs on the JVM and gives you easy access to any existing Java library.

If you have ever programmed in a Lisp, you will know that lists are at the core of the language. Clojure extends this and puts an abstraction on lists so that data structures are at the core of the language—not only lists but vectors, sets, and maps. All of these are represented in the syntax, and the code of a Clojure program is in fact both written and represented internally using these data structures. In comparison to the data structures you might be used to from other languages, these structures cannot be modified. Instead, you change them by describing a change, and you will get back a new data structure. The old one still exists and can be used. This all must sound very wasteful, and it's true that it's not as efficient as bashing bits in place. But it's not as slow as you would expect—Clojure has extremely mature and clever implementations of these data structures. And the benefits of this immutability make it possible for Clojure to do things that most other languages can't easily do. Immutable data structures have another strong benefit: since you never modify them in place, they are always thread safe, without you having to do anything at all.

One of the main reasons people are turning to Clojure right now is that it has a very well-thought-out model for how to handle concurrency and parallel execution. The basic idea is that in Clojure everything is immutable. But you can create a few different kinds of structures that make it possible to do what looks like mutation. The structure you choose depends on what kind of control you want to exert over the mutation.

Say you want to make sure three variables all change at the same time, without anyone seeing any of them in an inconsistent state. You can achieve this by making the variables be saved in refs and then use Clojure's Software Transactional Memory (STM) to coordinate access to them.

All in all, Clojure has many nice things going for it. It's very pragmatic in its interoperability with Java. It gives you complete control over the concurrent aspects of your program, without requiring error-prone approaches such as locks or mutexes.

Now let's see what actual Clojure code looks like. The first example is a simple "Hello, World" program. Just like many so-called scripting languages, Clojure will execute anything at the top level. The following code will first define a function named (hello) and then call it with two different arguments:

MostInterestingLanguages/clojure/hello.clj
```
(defn hello [name]
  (println "Hello" name))

(hello "Ola")
(hello "Stella")
```

If you have a clj command defined, you can run this file and get this expected response:

```
$ clj hello.clj
Hello Ola
Hello Stella
```

As mentioned, it's very easy to work with data structures in Clojure, and you can do very powerful things with them. Here is a small example of how to create the different data structures and then take something out of them:

MostInterestingLanguages/clojure/data_structures.clj

```clojure
(def a_value 42)

(def a_list '(55 24 10))

(def a_vector [1 1 2 3 5])

(def a_map {:one 1 :two 2 :three 3, :four 4})

(def a_set #{1 2 3})

(println (first a_list))
(println (nth a_vector 4))
(println (:three a_map))
(println (contains? a_set 3))

(let [[x y z] a_list]
  (println x)
  (println y)
  (println z))
```

The most interesting part of this code is what happens on the last few lines. The let statement allow us to destructure a collection into its component parts. This example just takes a list of three elements apart and assigns them to x, y, and z, but Clojure actually allows arbitrary nesting and destructuring of collections like this.

When run, the code will result in output like this:

```
$ clj data_structures.clj
55
5
3
true
55
24
10
```

When working with Clojure data collections, you generally add or remove elements and then use the new collection created by doing this. No matter what collection you use, Clojure supports three functions on it that give you most of what you actually need. These functions are (count), (conj), and (seq). The (count) function is pretty self-explanatory. Calling (conj) with a collection will allow you to add something to that collection, depending on where it is appropriate for that collection to add things. So, using (conj) to add something to a List will put the added element at the front of the list. For Vector, it will be put last. And for a Map, (conj) will add a key-value pair.

To work with a collection in a generic way, Clojure supports an abstraction called Sequence. Any collection can be turned into a Sequence by calling (seq). Once you have a Sequence, you will be able to traverse the collection using (first) and (rest).

So, what does this look like in practice?

MostInterestingLanguages/clojure/data_structures2.clj
```
(def a_list '(1 2 3 4))
(def a_map {:foo 42 :bar 12})

(println (first a_list))
(println (rest a_list))

(println (first a_map))
(println (rest a_map))

(def another_map (conj a_map [:quux 32]))

(println a_map)
(println another_map)
```

In this code, I first print the first and remaining parts of a list and a map. Then I create a new map by adding a key-value binding to an existing map. The original map remains unchanged, as can be seen if we execute this code:

```
$ clj data_structures2.clj
1
(2 3 4)
[:foo 42]
([:bar 12])
{:foo 42, :bar 12}
{:foo 42, :quux 32, :bar 12}
```

Clojure has a really good relationship with Java. In fact, it is sometimes hard to see where the Java ends and the Clojure begins. For example, we talked about the Sequence abstraction earlier. This is really just a Java interface. Interoperating with Java libraries is usually as simple as just calling it.

MostInterestingLanguages/clojure/java_interop.clj
```
(def a_hash_map (new java.util.HashMap))
(def a_tree_map (java.util.TreeMap.))

(println a_hash_map)
(.put a_hash_map "foo" "42")
(.put a_hash_map "bar" "46")

(println a_hash_map)
(println (first a_hash_map))
(println (.toUpperCase "hello"))
```

Any Java class on the classpath can easily be instantiated, either by calling (new) and giving the class an argument or by using the special form where the name of the class with a dot at the end is used as a function. After we have a Java instance, we can work with it just like any other Clojure object. We can also call Java methods on the object, using the special syntax where the method name begins with a dot. Calling Java methods this way is not restricted to things created from Java classes. In fact, a Clojure string is just a regular Java string, so you can call toUpperCase() on it directly.

This code would result in the following output:

```
$ clj java_interop.clj
#<HashMap {}>
#<HashMap {foo=42, bar=46}>
#<Entry foo=42>
HELLO
```

Seeing as I've mentioned the concurrency aspects of Clojure, I wanted to show you what using the STM looks like. It sounds very daunting, but it's actually quite simple to use in practice.

MostInterestingLanguages/clojure/stm.clj
```
(defn transfer [from to amount]
  (dosync
   (alter from #(- % amount))
   (alter to #(+ % amount))
   )
  )

(def ola_balance (ref 42))
(def matt_balance (ref 4000))

(println @ola_balance @matt_balance)

(transfer matt_balance ola_balance 200)

(println @ola_balance @matt_balance)

(transfer ola_balance matt_balance 2)

(println @ola_balance @matt_balance)
```

There are several things going on in this example, but the things to notice are (ref), (dosync), and (alter). The code creates a new reference by calling (ref) and giving it the initial value. The at sign is used to get the current value out of the reference. Anything that happens inside the (dosync) block will happen inside a transaction, which means that no code will ever be able to see the parts involved in an inconsistent state.

However, in order to make that possible, (dosync) might execute its code more than once. The calls to (alter) are how the actual references get changed. The funky syntax with the octothorpe (hash) sign is how you create an anonymous function in Clojure.

When running this code, we get the expected output. This code doesn't actually use any threads, but we can depend on the result of this no matter how many threads were bouncing on these references.

```
$ clj stm.clj
42 4000
242 3800
240 3802
```

There are many other features of Clojure I wish I could show you in this section, but at this point we have to continue to the next language. Look up the following resources to get a good grounding in the language. I highly recommend it—it's a real pleasure to work with.

Resources

Several books about Clojure are available. *Programming Clojure [Hal09]* by Stuart Halloway was the first one and is still a good introduction to the language. The second edition, coauthored by Aaron Bedra, has just been released.

I'm also a fan of *The Joy of Clojure [FH11]* for learning how to write idiomatic Clojure.

When it comes to getting a good grounding in the full language, I like the Clojure home page (http://clojure.org). It has good reference material, and you can pick up a lot about Clojure from just looking through the articles there.

Finally, the mailing list is a crucial aid in learning. It's a very active list, and you regularly see Clojure core people answering questions. This is also where many discussions about upcoming features in Clojure will be discussed.

CoffeeScript

In the past few years, JavaScript has seen a large uptick in popularity. A major reason for this is that more and more companies are working with HTML5 as the main delivery mechanism of applications, and it has become necessary to create better user interfaces for web applications. To make this happen, more and more JavaScript has to be written, but there is a huge problem with this, namely, that JavaScript can sometimes be very hard to get right. It has a tricky object model, and the way it works doesn't always make sense on the surface. Its syntax can also be very clunky.

Enter CoffeeScript.

CoffeeScript is a relatively new language, but it's already ranked on GitHub as one of the most interesting projects there. It is also the odd man (woman?) out in this collection of languages, since it isn't really a full language. It is more like a thin layer on top of JavaScript—it actually compiles down to quite readable JavaScript. It takes a lot of inspiration from both Ruby and Python, and if you have used either of those languages, you should feel mostly at home with CoffeeScript.

CoffeeScript uses indentation for structuring a program, just like Python. One of the main goals of the language is to be more readable and easier to work with than JavaScript, and a huge part of that is syntax.

But CoffeeScript isn't only about syntax, although syntax is a large part. It also supports advanced features such as comprehensions and pattern matching.

CoffeeScript also gives some basic syntax to make it easier to set up classlike hierarchies. One of the more annoying aspects of JavaScript is how to stitch things together so you get the correct inheritance structure. CoffeeScript make this easy, especially when coming from another language with a standard class-based object-oriented system.

At the end of the day, CoffeeScript won't give you any major new capabilities, but it will make writing the JavaScript side of your application a bit easier. It will also make your JavaScript code more consistent and easier to read and maintain.

Let's get started! A simple CoffeeScript "Hello, World" program could look like this:

```
MostInterestingLanguages/coffee_script/hello.coffee
greeting = "hello: "
hello = (name) =>
    console.log greeting + name

hello "Ola"
hello "Stella"
```

If you have CoffeeScript installed with Node.js, you can run it like this:

```
$ coffee hello.coffee
hello: Ola
hello: Stella
```

As you can see from this simple example, the method we create is a lexical closure, using the greeting variable. We don't need to use parentheses, just as in Ruby. The parser tries to make things as easy as possible for us.

CoffeeScript makes it really easy to create nested objects. Either you can do that using explicit delimiters or you can use indentation to mark when something starts and ends.

MostInterestingLanguages/coffee_script/nested_objects.coffee
```
words = ["foo", "bar", "quux"]
numbers = {One: 1, Three: 3, Four: 4}

sudoku = [
    4, 3, 5
    6, 8, 2
    1, 9, 7
]

languages =
    ruby:
        creator: "Matz"
        appeared: 1995

    clojure:
        creator: "Rich Hickey"
        appeared: 2007

console.log words
console.log numbers
console.log sudoku
console.log languages
```

When running this, you get the following:

```
$ coffee nested_objects.coffee
[ 'foo', 'bar', 'quux' ]
{ One: 1, Three: 3, Four: 4 }
[ 4, 3, 5, 6, 8, 2, 1, 9, 7 ]
{ ruby: { creator: 'Matz', appeared: 1995 }
, clojure: { creator: 'Rich Hickey', appeared: 2007 }
}
```

It makes me a bit sad when printed output is less clean than the statements that created it. But I guess that's one of the benefits of CoffeeScript—being able to create these nested objects really cleanly.

One of the advantages of CoffeeScript is the ability to define comprehensions over objects. You do that using the for keyword.

MostInterestingLanguages/coffee_script/comprehensions.coffee

```
values =
    for x in [1..100] by 2 when 1000 < x*x*x < 10000
        [x, x*x*x]

console.log values
```

When running this code, you will get all the even numbers between 1 and 100 whose cubes are between 1,000 and 10,000.

```
$ coffee comprehensions.coffee
[ [ 11, 1331 ]
, [ 13, 2197 ]
, [ 15, 3375 ]
, [ 17, 4913 ]
, [ 19, 6859 ]
, [ 21, 9261 ]
]
```

CoffeeScript comprehensions not only make it possible to do many collection operations on lists and ranges but also work well on objects and dictionaries.

MostInterestingLanguages/coffee_script/classes.coffee

```
class Component
    constructor: (@name) ->

    print: ->
        console.log "component #{@name}"

class Label extends Component
    constructor: (@title) ->
        super "Label: #{@title}"

    print: ->
        console.log @title

class Composite extends Component
    constructor: (@objects...) ->
        super "composite"
    print: ->
        console.log "["
        object.print() for object in @objects
        console.log "]"

l1 = new Label "hello"
l2 = new Label "goodbye"
l3 = new Label "42"

new Composite(l1, l3, l2).print()
```

This final example shows how CoffeeScript makes it possible to create a more traditional object-oriented structure for your programs if that's what suits your problem. If you are used to the way Java or Ruby works, the behavior of CoffeeScript's constructors and super won't come as any surprise. The previous program results in this output:

```
$ coffee classes.coffee
[
hello
42
goodbye
]
```

If you have ever used and disliked JavaScript, CoffeeScript should come as a welcome relief. It's possible to use both on the server side and on the client side, and Rails now bundles CoffeeScript. You should definitely give it a go!

Resources

The best way to start with CoffeeScript is http://coffeescript.org. This site has a nice overview of all the major language features. It also sports an interactive console where you can type in CoffeeScript code and immediately see the JavaScript it gets translated into.

The *CoffeeScript [Bur11]* book by Trevor Burnham is also a good resource.

If you like to learn programming languages by example, the home page also has annotated source code for much of the internals. This makes it even easier to read and understand what's going on.

Erlang

Erlang is the oldest language in this list, having been around since the late 1980s. However, it is just recently that people have really started to take notice of it.

Erlang was created by Joe Armstrong to make it possible to write fault-tolerant programs. The main domain for Erlang was for long-distance telephone switches and other domains where uptime is the most important thing. Most of the other features of Erlang come out of the requirements for code to be robust, fault tolerant, and possible to swap out at runtime.

The reason Erlang is seeing more and more use in other domains is that the underlying actor model of the language makes it a very good fit for creating robust and scalable servers.

Erlang is a functional language. Functions are first-class things that can be created when necessary, passed around as arguments, and returned from other functions. Erlang allows you to assign a name only once—giving you immutability.

The core model of Erlang is the Actor model. The idea is that you can have loads of small processes (called *actors*) that can communicate with each other only by sending messages. So in Erlang, the way you model behavior and changing state is with actors. If you have worked with threads or processes in other languages, it's important to remember that Erlang processes are quite different: they are very small and fast to create, and you can distribute them to different physical machines if you want. This makes it possible to write your program the same way, whether it should run on one machine or on a hundred machines.

Tightly entwined with Erlang is the Open Telecom Platform (OTP), which is a set of libraries that can be used to create very robust servers. It gives the programmer a framework to hook into some of the more advanced patterns for creating reliable Erlang servers—such as actors monitoring other actors' health, easy hotswapping of code in running actors, and many other powerful features.

In comparison to the languages we have seen so far, Erlang can't run from the top level of a script, so I will instead show you executing code from Erlang's console. One side effect of this is that the simplest program we write is slightly longer, since we have to expose it as an Erlang module.

MostInterestingLanguages/erlang/hello.erl
```
-module(hello).
-export([hello/1]).

hello(Name) ->
    io:format("Hello ~s~n", [Name]).
```

The first two lines are directives that export information about the module we are writing. We define a function called hello(). Variables have to start with a capital letter, as you can see with Name. The format() function lives in the io module and can do pretty flexible formatting. For our purposes now, we interpolate only the name in the string and print it.

When executing this code in the Erlang shell, it looks like this:

```
1> c(hello).
{ok,hello}
2> hello:hello("Ola").
Hello Ola
```

```
ok
3> hello:hello("Stella").
Hello Stella
ok
```

Every Erlang statement ends with a period to tell the interpreter we are done. Before we can use a module, we have to compile it, which we do with the c() function. After that, we can call the module. The ok value is the return value of the function we created.

Erlang is a functional language, and one of its really strong sides is support for pattern matching and recursive algorithms. Before looking at the next example, it's good to know that names that begin with lowercase letters are symbols in Erlang. Anything inside curly braces is a tuple, and square brackets are lists. These three combine to form the different kinds of things you generally pattern match on in Erlang.

MostInterestingLanguages/erlang/patterns.erl
```erlang
-module(patterns).
-export([run/0]).

run() ->
    io:format("- ~s~n", [pattern_in_func("something")]),
    io:format("- ~w~n", [pattern_in_func({foo, 43})]),
    io:format("- ~w~n", [pattern_in_func({foo, 42})]),
    io:format("- ~s~n", [pattern_in_func([])]),
    io:format("- ~s~n", [pattern_in_func(["foo"])]),
    io:format("- ~s~n", [pattern_in_func(["foo", "bar"])]),
    io:format("- ~w~n", [pattern_in_case()]),
    io:format("- ~w~n", [reverse([1,2,3])]),
    io:format("- ~w~n", [reverse([])])
    .

pattern_in_func({foo, 43}) ->
    23;
pattern_in_func({foo, Value}) ->
    Value + 10;
pattern_in_func([]) ->
    "Empty list";
pattern_in_func([H|[]]) ->
    "List with one element";
pattern_in_func(X) ->
    "Something else".

pattern_in_case() ->
    case {42, [55, 60]} of
        {55, [42 | Rest]} -> {rest, Rest};
        {42, [55 | Rest]} -> {something, Rest}
    end.
```

```
reverse(L) ->
    reverse(L, []).

reverse([], Accum) ->
    Accum;

reverse([H|T], Accum) ->
    reverse(T, [H] ++ Accum).
```

This code first creates a run() method that will exercise the different things defined in this module. There are three different ways of doing pattern matching with Erlang, the first being in function arguments, the second in case statements, and the third when working with message passing. The previous code shows only the two first versions. It also shows how a tail-recursive algorithm can be easily written using Erlang's pattern matching facilities.

```
18> c(patterns).
{ok,patterns}
19> patterns:run().
- Something else
- 23
- 52
- Empty list
- List with one element
- Something else
- {something,[60]}
- [3,2,1]
- []
ok
```

The syntax where a pipe is used inside a list allow us to separate the head of the list from the rest of it. It's a very common pattern in many functional languages to separate the head from the tail and then do something with either. In the case of the reverse() function, I just put the head and the tail back together in a different order.

The main thing Erlang is known for is its support for actors. In the next example, we will see a very simple actor that just contains some state. This is more or less akin to a synchronized memory area that will always be internally consistent. The main syntax necessary to understand here is the exclamation mark, which is used to send a message to an actor. You can send any serializable Erlang term to an actor—including functions. The receive keyword is used much like a case statement, except that it will wait for messages coming to the current actor running.

MostInterestingLanguages/erlang/actor.erl

```erlang
-module(actor).
-export([run/0]).

run() ->
    State1 = spawn(fun() -> state(42) end),
    State2 = spawn(fun() -> state(2000) end),
    io:format("State1 ~w~n", [get_from(State1)]),
    io:format("State2 ~w~n", [get_from(State2)]),

    State1 ! {inc}, State1 ! {inc},
    State2 ! {inc}, State2 ! {inc}, State2 ! {inc},

    io:format("State1 ~w~n", [get_from(State1)]),
    io:format("State2 ~w~n", [get_from(State2)]),

    State1 ! {update, fun(Value) -> Value * 100 end},

    io:format("State1 ~w~n", [get_from(State1)]),
    io:format("State2 ~w~n", [get_from(State2)])
    .

get_from(State) ->
    State ! {self(), get},
    receive
        Value ->
            Value
    end.

state(Value) ->
    receive
        {From, get} ->
            From ! Value,
            state(Value);
        {inc} ->
            state(Value + 1);
        {From, cas, OldValue, NewValue} ->
            case Value of
                {OldValue} ->
                    From ! {set, NewValue},
                    state(NewValue);
                _ ->
                    From ! {notset, Value},
                    state(Value)
            end;
        {update, Func} ->
            state(Func(Value))
    end.
```

This code defines three different functions. The first one is used to run the actual example. It works by calling spawn two times, creating two different state actors. An actor is basically just a running function, so this code uses the fun keyword to create an anonymous function with the initial values of 42 and 2000. The code then gets the initial values and prints them. After that, it increments the first state two times and the second state three times and then prints them again. Finally, it sends a function to the actor to generate a new value by multiplying the old one by 100. Finally, it prints the values again. The second function is get_from(), which is a helper method to make it easier to get the values out of the actor. It works by sending a get message to the actor given as an argument and then waits to receive an answer.

The final function is the actual actor. It works by waiting for messages and then does different things depending on which message it receives. It calls itself recursively after it's done and can in that way keep state.

```
32> c(actor).
{ok,actor}
33> actor:run().
State1 42
State2 2000
State1 44
State2 2003
State1 4400
State2 2003
ok
```

Don't worry if you have to look at the final example for a while to see what is going on. The way state is handled is pretty different from most programming languages. Suffice to say, Erlang gives you very powerful primitives to work with concurrency, and the way you can compose and work with actors gives rise to extremely nice algorithms.

Resources

The best way to get started with Erlang is probably *Programming Erlang* [Arm07] by Joe Armstrong. It gives you a good grounding in the different aspects of the language, without shying away from some of the more complicated aspects of it. Another good book is *Erlang Programming [CT09]* by Francesco Cesarini and Simon Thompson.

You can also get started with Erlang from several sources on the Web. In that case, http://learnyousomeerlang.com is a good resource.

Factor

Factor was created in 2003, inspired by the much older language Forth. It is a stack-oriented programming language, which makes the programming model very different from what most programmers are used to using. During Factor's evolution, the way you work with it has changed substantially. The language used to be based on the JVM but is now implemented mostly in itself and runs on all major platforms.

The programming model of a stack-based language is deceptively simple. Everything you do works on a stack. Every operation can take and/or put values on this stack, and in most cases this happens implicitly. So, to add two numbers together, you first push the two numbers on the stack and then execute the plus() word. This will take the numbers from the top of the stack and push back the result. Stack-based languages use the stack for many things that other languages use variables for. In most cases, a stack-based language will also use the stack to send arguments to functions.

Factor has a large set of libraries that come with the standard distribution, and the language itself also contains many advanced features, such as a class system, tuple classes, macros, user-defined parsing words, and a very competent foreign function interface.

The syntax of the language is very simple, using reverse Polish notation. It usually takes some time to get used to, but after a while it becomes very natural, and it allows you to follow the operations on the stack in an obvious way.

```
MostInterestingLanguages/factor/hello.factor
USE: io
USE: kernel
USE: sequences
IN: user

: hello ( x -- ) "hello " swap append print ;

"Ola" hello
"Stella" hello
```

This code is the equivalent of the "Hello, World" code we've seen before. We begin by defining the modules we want to use and state that we are in the user vocabulary via IN: user. We define a new word called hello() by beginning a line with colon. Inside the parentheses, we say that the stack effect of this word is to take one element and not put anything back. Finally, we push the string *hello* and then swap the two strings on top of the stack, append them together, and finally print the result. After the word is defined, we can call it after pushing a string on the stack.

If you have Factor on your command line, the result of running this file is just as expected.

```
$ factor hello.factor
hello Ola
hello Stella
```

The way you think about Factor code is fundamentally different, because you usually need to keep track of what's currently on the stack. You also have to make sure everything bottoms out correctly. Factor will not accept a program where the end result is not what it expects. That's one of the main reasons words will define what their input and output on the stack are.

The next example shows several different small programs that do things easily with Factor:

```
MostInterestingLanguages/factor/parsing_passwd.factor
USE: io
USE: io.encodings.utf8
USE: io.files
USE: kernel
USE: math
USE: sequences
USE: splitting
USE: xml.syntax
USE: xml.writer
IN: user

3 [ "Hello" print ] times

{ "foo" "bar" "baz" }
[ [XML <li><-></li> XML] ] map
[XML <ul><-></ul> XML] pprint-xml

nl nl

: separate-lines ( seq -- seq2 ) [ ":" split first ] map ;
: remove-comments ( seq -- seq2 ) [ "#" head? not ] filter ;
: remove-underscore-names ( seq -- seq2 ) [ "_" head? not ] filter ;

"/etc/passwd" utf8 file-lines
    separate-lines remove-comments remove-underscore-names
    [ print ] each
```

The first section of the program (after the use statements) prints *hello* three times to the console, by first pushing the number 3 and then a so-called quotation. A Factor quotation is basically an anonymous function. In this case, the quotation will just print *hello*, but it could also use values from the stack or push values as side effects. Finally, the word times() is called, which actually will execute the block three times.

The second part shows a very powerful aspect of Factor—you can create your own parser words to define specialized syntax. Factor includes lots of different variations on this already. This example shows XML literal syntax. However, this syntax is not built into the language; it's defined as a library. In this segment, I first push a list of three elements, then create XML fragments out of each of them using map(), and finally pretty print it using pprint-xml().

The final section first defines a few helper words called separate-lines(), remove-comments(), and remove-underscore-names(). These are used to read all the lines from the /etc/passwd file, split all the columns, and retain only the usernames that don't start with underscores. Finally, it prints all of these.

When running this file, you get the following output—depending on what's in your password file, of course:

```
$ factor parsing_passwd.factor
Hello
Hello
Hello

<ul>
  <li>
    foo
  </li>
  <li>
    bar
  </li>
  <li>
    baz
  </li>
</ul>

nobody
root
daemon
```

If you are familiar with object-oriented languages, much Factor code almost looks like you are calling methods on things over and over again. Viewing it that way can lead to misunderstandings, since any word can touch anything that's on the stack so far. That is one of the main reasons why Factor, while a very small language, makes it very easy to create reusable and composable components.

Resources

The Factor home page at http://factorcode.org really has all the resources you could want. It contains lots of articles about the language, pointers to good blog posts, and also a large amount of example code. If you refresh the front page, you will see different code examples show up, all of them eminently understandable and all very small.

Slava Pestov, the creator of Factor, has also done several talks about Factor, and many of these can easily be found online.

Finally, the Factor development environment allows you to easily find new information about what's going on; it also contains the source code for itself and a large amount of the language. Just sitting down with it will teach you a lot about Factor.

Fantom

Fantom is a relatively new language. It used to be called Fan, but the name was changed a few years ago. It's a language that runs on the JVM and the CLR. The goal of the language is to be able to write code that runs well on both platforms, while solving many of the problems with Java and C#. It's a very pragmatic language; it doesn't try to revolutionize either syntax or libraries or type systems. It just tries to improve on the current situation, creating a language that makes it easier to get things done.

Since Fantom has to run seamlessly on several platforms, the libraries have been designed from the ground up to abstract away any Java or C#-specific parts. In many other regards, Fantom is quite similar to Java or C#. It is a curly brace language. It is statically typed—but it doesn't have generics. The creators of Fantom rejected them for making the type system too complex and have instead created specific solutions for collection classes. Being statically typed, it requires you to annotate methods and fields with their types. However, type inference is used for local variables and collection literals to make them easier to work with.

Fantom has some fancy features that allow you to go around the static type system if you really want. You can make dynamic calls to any object, but that uses a different syntax than regular method calls. This, plus really nice metaprogramming facilities, makes it possible to write powerful and succinct programs in Fantom.

Another feature that Fantom promotes is the notion of modularity. Fantom gives you several different ways of modeling the relationships between classes.

You can use mixins, but you can also use functions or actors if that makes more sense.

In many regards, Fantom is a bit to Java like CoffeeScript is to JavaScript. It tries to clean up some of the things that might not have been such a good idea, redesign the libraries from scratch to be more consistent and easier to work with, and add features that Java should have had a long time ago, such as mixins and closures. Programming in Fantom feels pretty much like home if you're used to Java or C#, except that a few nice things have been added to decrease the lines of code you have to write.

Just as with our other languages, we'll start with a simple "Hello, World" example.

```
MostInterestingLanguages/fantom/hello.fan
class HelloWorld {
    static Void main() {
        hw := HelloWorld()
        hw.hello("Ola")
        hw.hello("Stella")
    }

    Void hello(Str name) {
        echo("hello $name")
    }
}
```

There are some things to note here. First, everything is wrapped in a class, just as in Java or C#. This class has a main() method that will get called when this program is run. I create a new instance of the HelloWorld class by just naming the class and putting parentheses on it. Fantom actually has named constructors, but the default name is make(), which will get called automatically if you just use the class name as a method call. I create a variable called hw. The := syntax tells Fantom to infer the type of the variable. I then call hello() two times with different arguments. Notice that there are no semicolons to end statements. The hello() method takes one argument and echoes it out to the screen, with *hello* prepended to it. Fantom has a shorthand for interpolating strings, using the dollar sign.

When run, this code generates the expected result:

```
$ fan hello.fan
hello Ola
hello Stella
```

As I mentioned, Fantom doesn't really have user-defined generic types like Java and C#. Instead, it supports generics only for some collection types and for defining closures.

```
MostInterestingLanguages/fantom/generic.fan
class Generic {
    static Void main() {
        list_of_ints := Int[1, 2, 3, 4]
        another_list := [1, 1, 2, 3, 5]
        empty_int_list := Int[,]
        empty_obj_list := [,]

        list3 := [1, 1, null, 3, 5]

        echo(Type.of(list_of_ints))
        echo(Type.of(another_list))
        echo(Type.of(empty_int_list))
        echo(Type.of(empty_obj_list))
        echo(Type.of(list3))

        map := ["one": 1, "two": 2, "three": 3]
        map2 := Int:Str[42: "answer", 26: "question"]
        empty_map := [:]
        empty_int_map := Int:Int[:]

        echo(Type.of(map))
        echo(Type.of(map2))
        echo(Type.of(empty_map))
        echo(Type.of(empty_int_map))
    }
}
```

This code will create a few different examples of generic lists and generic maps. If you don't provide a type when creating a list or map, Fantom will figure out what type to use itself. One of the interesting Fantom features that can be seen here is the concept of nullable types. By default, no variable can contain null in Fantom. However, if you put a question mark after the type name, then that variable can contain either values of that type or null. This makes non-null values the default and thus makes many common bugs impossible. The same is true for lists and maps. By default, type inference will not give them a nullable type, but if you have a null somewhere when creating the literal, the type will be assumed to be nullable.

If we run this code, we'll see that the variable types match what we would expect:

```
$ fan generic.fan
sys::Int[]
sys::Int[]
sys::Int[]
sys::Obj?[]
sys::Int?[]
[sys::Str:sys::Int]
[sys::Int:sys::Str]
[sys::Obj:sys::Obj?]
[sys::Int:sys::Int]
```

Fantom supports lightweight closures and function types. In many cases, you work with them just like you work with blocks in Ruby, with the difference that you easily can send in more than one block to a function. If you don't define an argument list for a closure, it will assume an implicit variable called it. You can call a closure by just referring to it with parentheses after the name, just as with a regular method call.

The Fantom standard library contains many of the things you would expect to find there if you've worked in a dynamic language like Ruby or Groovy.

MostInterestingLanguages/fantom/closures.fan
```
class Closures {
    static Void main() {
        h := |name| { echo("Hello $name") }
        h("Ola")
        h("Stella")

        list := [42, 12, 56456, 23476]
        list2 := ["Fox", "Quux", "Bar", "Blarg", "Aardvark"]

        list.each { echo("Number $it") }

        echo(list2.sort |left, right| { right.size <=> left.size })
    }
}
```

Here we first create a closure from scratch. It takes one argument. We then call it with two different names. After that, we create a list of ints and a list of strings. The each() method allows you to iterate over a collection of things. Here you can see how we use the implicit it variable instead of defining an argument name. The second example takes two arguments and sorts a list based on what the closure returns. This is very similar to a Java Comparator.

When we run this code, it looks like this:

```
$ fan closures.fan
Hello Ola
Hello Stella
Number 42
Number 12
Number 56456
Number 23476
[Aardvark, Blarg, Quux, Fox, Bar]
```

Although Fantom uses strong static typing in most cases, Fantom also has a lightweight way of getting around it, by supporting dynamic invocation. If you make a call using the -> operator instead of the dot, you will make a dynamic call that the type checker won't notice. If the method exists on the target object, it will be called just as if you had called it with static typing. However, you can also hook in to the process that decides what happens on a dynamic call by overriding a method called trap(). By doing that, you can emulate some very fancy things from the dynamic language community, without losing type safety in other parts of your application.

The following example makes it possible to generate XML using method calls and closures:

MostInterestingLanguages/fantom/dynamic.fan

```
class XmlBuilder {
    Str content
    Int indent
    new make() { this.content = ""; this.indent = 0 }

    override Obj? trap(Str name, Obj?[]? args) {
        this.content += "${doIndent()}<$name>\n"
        this.indent += 1
        if(args != null && args.size > 0) {
            if(args[0] is Func) {
                ((Func)args[0])(this)
            } else {
                this.content += doIndent()
                this.content += args[0]
                this.content += "\n"
            }
        }
        this.indent -= 1
        this.content += "${doIndent()}</$name>\n"
        return this.content
    }
    Str doIndent() {
        Str.spaces(this.indent * 2)
    }
}
```

```
class Dynamic {
    static Void main() {
        x := XmlBuilder()
        x->html {
            x->title("ThoughtWorks Anthology")
            x->body {
                x->h1("Welcome!")
            }
        }

        echo(x.content)
    }
}
```

The XmlBuilder class keeps track of the current content and the indentation level. It overrides the trap() method and inside of it does several things. It first prints an opening tag to the content string. It then changes the indentation level. After that, it checks whether it got any argument, and if it did, whether it's a function. If it's a function, we simply invoke it. If not, we just append the argument to the content string. Finally, we change the indent back and close the tag.

With this machinery in place, the main() method can very easily create an XML document by calling made-up method names on the XmlBuilder instance. When we run this code, it executes as we expect.

```
$ fan dynamic.fan
<html>
  <title>
    ThoughtWorks Anthology
  </title>
  <body>
    <h1>
      Welcome!
    </h1>
  </body>
</html>
```

Fantom is a very powerful language. It hides the power a bit behind curly-brace syntax, but once you get beyond that, you can do anything you could do in Java or C# but in a clearer and cleaner way. You also get portability between platforms as an added bonus.

Resources

One problem with Fantom is that it doesn't have that many resources. The home page at http://fantom.org covers some of what you might want. There is also an IRC channel at Freenode.

These resources take you some distance, but I had to do a lot of digging when first learning the language, and you might have to, too. However, it's well worth it.

Haskell

Of all the functional languages on this list, Haskell can definitely be said to take the functional paradigm the furthest. Haskell is a pure functional programming language, which means the language doesn't support mutability or side effects in any way. Of course, that's a truth with modification, since if it truly didn't support any side effects, you couldn't get it to print anything or take input from a user. Haskell does make it possible to do I/O and things that look like side effects, but in the language model, no side effects are actually occurring.

Another aspect that makes Haskell a fundamentally different language is that it's a lazy language. That means arguments to functions aren't evaluated until they are actually needed. This makes it really easy to do things such as create infinite streams, recursive function definitions, and many other useful things. Since there are no side effects, you usually won't notice that Haskell is lazy, unless you specifically utilize this aspect of the language.

Ever since ML, functional programming languages have branched into two different families of languages—the ones that use static typing and the ones that don't. Haskell is one of the more advanced statically typed functional languages, and its type system can express many things that are hard to express in other languages. However, even though the type system is very capable, it usually doesn't intrude much when actually writing a program. In most cases, you don't have to put types on functions or names; Haskell will use type inference to figure out the correct types by itself.

Haskell does not have a type system with inheritance. Instead, it uses generics to a large degree. A big part of this system is due to something called *type classes*. These classes allow you to add polymorphic behavior to existing types. You can think of type classes as interfaces with implementations that can be added to a class after it's been defined. It's a very powerful feature of Haskell, and once you start using it, you will miss it in other languages.

All in all, Haskell is a very powerful language. It is used by researchers to push the borders in many different areas, which means many new interesting libraries will first be available in Haskell. As an example, Haskell has support for many different concurrency paradigms, including Software Transactional Memory (STM) and nested data parallelism.

It is kind of weird to start a code example of Haskell with a "Hello, World"
example, since the things that make it possible to create I/O in Haskell have
a tendency to complicate things a bit. But no matter, let's see what it looks
like.

MostInterestingLanguages/haskell/hello.hs
```
module Main where

main = do
  hello "Ola"
  hello "Stella"

hello name = putStrLn ("Hello " ++ name)
```

To run this as a stand-alone file, we have to define a main() function inside a
module called Main. The do keyword allow us to do several things after each
other. Finally, we define hello() to be a function that takes one argument,
concatenates that argument with "Hello ", and then prints it.

When we compile and run this code, it looks like this:

```
$ ghc -o hello hello.hs
$ ./hello
Hello Ola
Hello Stella
```

Just as with Erlang, Haskell is really good at pattern matching. I haven't
mentioned it yet, but Haskell is a whitespace-significant language, which
means it uses whitespace to determine structure, just like CoffeeScript and
Python. When it comes to pattern matching, this results in quite clean-looking
programs. The following creates a data type for representing shapes and then
uses pattern matching to calculate the area for different shapes. It also
revisits our example of reversing a list by recursion and pattern matching.

MostInterestingLanguages/haskell/patterns.hs
```
module Main where

type Radius = Double
type Side   = Double

data Shape =
          Point
        | Circle    Radius
        | Rectangle Side Side
        | Square    Side
area Point          = 0
area (Circle r)     = pi * r * r
area (Rectangle w h) = w * h
area (Square s)     = s * s
```

```
rev [] = []
rev (x:xs) = rev xs ++ [x]

main = do
  print (area Point)
  print (area (Circle 10))
  print (area (Rectangle 20 343535))
  print (area (Square 20))
  print (rev [42, 55, 10, 20])
```

This gives the following output:

```
$ ghc -o patterns patterns.hs
$ ./patterns
0.0
314.1592653589793
6870700.0
400.0
[20,10,55,42]
```

As you can see, most function definitions in Haskell look a lot like algebraic statements. When defining a data type like Shape, we enumerate all the possibilities and say what data the possibilities must take. Then, when we dispatch based on the data in the call to area(), we also pick out the data contained in the data type.

I mentioned earlier that Haskell is a lazy language. That can be easily demonstrated when defining something that works with infinity, for example.

MostInterestingLanguages/haskell/lazy.hs
```
module Main where

from n = n : (from (n + 1))

main = do
  print (take 10 (from 20))
```

This code looks deceptively simple. The take() function is defined in the Haskell core library. It will take as many elements from the given list as you specify (ten in this case). Our function from() uses the colon to construct a new list. That list is defined as the value of n and then the list you get from calling from() again, with n + 1. In most languages, any time you call this function, it will recurse forever, and that's game over. But Haskell will evaluate from() only enough times to get the values it needs. This is pretty deep stuff and usually takes some time to sink in. Just remember, there is nothing special with the colon operator here. It's just the way Haskell evaluates things.

The result of running the code looks like this:

```
$ ghc -o lazy lazy.hs
$ ./lazy
[20,21,22,23,24,25,26,27,28,29]
```

The final thing I wanted to show about Haskell is something called *type
classes*. Since Haskell is not object-oriented and doesn't have inheritance, it
becomes really cumbersome to do things such as define a generic function
that can print things, test equality, or do a range of other things. Type classes
solve this problem, by basically allowing you to switch implementations based
on what type Haskell thinks something is. This can be extremely powerful
and very unlike anything you've seen in traditional object-oriented languages.
So, let's take a look at an example.

MostInterestingLanguages/haskell/type_classes.hs
```
module Main where

type Name = String

data Platypus =
    Platypus Name
data Bird =
    Pochard Name
  | RingedTeal Name
  | WoodDuck Name

class Duck d where
  quack :: d -> IO ()
  walk  :: d -> IO ()

instance Duck Platypus where
    quack (Platypus name) = putStrLn ("QUACK from Mr Platypus " ++ name)
    walk  (Platypus _) = putStrLn "*platypus waddle*"
instance Duck Bird where
    quack (Pochard name) = putStrLn ("(quack) says " ++ name)
    quack (RingedTeal name) = putStrLn ("QUACK!! says the Ringed Teal " ++ name)
    quack (WoodDuck _) = putStrLn "silence... "
    walk _ = putStrLn "*WADDLE*"

main = do
  quack (Platypus "Arnold")
  walk (Platypus "Arnold")
  quack (Pochard "Donald")
  walk (Pochard "Donald")
  quack (WoodDuck "Pelle")
  walk (WoodDuck "Pelle")
```

We have several things going on here. First, we define two data types: one for
birds and one for platypuses, which both receive names. Then we create a
type class called Duck. We know that if something quacks like a duck and

walks like a duck, it is a duck. So, the type class Duck defines two functions called quack() and walk(). These declarations specify only the types of the arguments and what return type is expected. These type signatures specify that they take a ducklike thing and then print something. After that, we define an instance of the type class for our Platypus. We simply define the functions necessary inside that instance, just as we would have when defining a top-level function in Haskell. Then we do the same thing for our birds, and finally we actually call quack() and walk() on a few different data instances.

When running this example, we see that it behaves exactly as we would want.

```
$ ghc -o type_classes type_classes.hs
$ ./type_classes
QUACK from Mr Platypus Arnold
*platypus waddle*
(quack) says Donald
*WADDLE*
silence...
*WADDLE*
```

Type classes are extremely powerful, and it's hard to do them justice in a small segment like this. Rest assured that once you fully understand type classes, then you are a good way toward mastery of Haskell.

Resources

The best place to start learning Haskell is an online book called *Learn You a Haskell for Great Good* (http://learnyouahaskell.com). This book will take you through the paces of Haskell in an easy and entertaining way.

There are several books covering Haskell, all of them approaching from slightly different angles. Many of them are focused on using Haskell from a math or computer science perspective. If you want to learn Haskell for general-purpose programming, the best book is probably *Real World Haskell [OGS08]* by Bryan O'Sullivan, Don Stewart, and John Goerzen. It's available online at http://book.realworldhaskell.org/read.

Io

Of all the languages in this essay, I think Io is my absolute favorite. It is a very small and powerful language. The core model is extremely regular and very simple, but it gives rise to many strange and wonderful features.

Io is a pure object-oriented programming language, where *pure* simply means that everything in Io is an object. No exceptions. Everything that you touch or work with or that the implementation uses is an object that you can reach in and get hold of. In comparison with Java, C#, Smalltalk, and many other object-oriented languages, Io does not use classes. Instead, it uses something called *prototype-based object orientation*. The idea is that you create a new object from an existing one. You make changes directly to the object and then use that as a basis for anything else.

Traditional object-oriented languages have two different concepts: classes and objects. In most pure languages, a class is a kind of object. But there is a fundamental difference between them, namely, that classes can hold behavior while objects can't. In Io, methods are objects, just like anything else, and methods can be added to any object. This programming model makes it possible to model things very differently from the way class-based languages require you to work. An additional advantage of prototype-based languages is that they can emulate class-based languages quite well. So, if you want to work with a more class-based model, you are free to do so.

Io is a small language, but it still supports a large chunk of functionality. It has some very nice concurrency features based on coroutines. Using Io actors, it's extremely easy to build robust and scalable concurrent programs.

Another aspect of Io being pure is that the elements that are used to represent Io code are available as first-class objects. This means you can create new code at runtime, you can modify existing code, and you can introspect on existing code. This makes it possible to create extraordinarily powerful metaprogramming programs.

In Io, you define a method just like you assign any other value. You create the method and assign it to a name. The first time you assign a name, you need to use :=, but after that, you can use =. Our "Hello, World" example looks like this:

```
MostInterestingLanguages/io/hello.io
hello := method(n,
  ("Hello " .. n) println)

hello("Ola")
hello("Stella")
```

We concatenate strings using the .. operator and print something by asking it to print itself. The output is highly unsurprising.

```
$ io hello.io
Hello Ola
Hello Stella
```

Io has cooperative multitasking using both actors and futures. Any object in Io can be used as an actor by calling asyncSend() to it, with the name of the

method to call. We do have to explicitly call yield to make sure all the code
gets to run.

```
MostInterestingLanguages/io/actors.io
t1 := Object clone do(
  test := method(
    for(n, 1, 5,
      n print
      yield))
)

t2 := t1 clone
t1 asyncSend(test)
t2 asyncSend(test)

10 repeat(yield)
"" println

t3 := Object clone do(
  test := method(
    "called" println
    wait(1)
    "after" println
    42))
result := t3 futureSend(test)
"we want the result now" println
result println
```

The first thing this code does is to create a new object called t1 with a test()
method that prints the numbers from one to five, yielding in between. We
then clone that object into another object and call asyncSend(test)() on both of
them, and finally we yield in the main thread ten times.

The second section creates a new object with another test() method that will
first print something and then wait for one second, print something else, and
then return a value. We can use this object as a transparent future by calling
futureSend(test)() to it. The result of that call won't be evaluated until we actually
have to use the value to print it, on the last line. This functionality is quite
similar to the way Haskell handles lazy values, but we have to explicitly create
the future to make this happen in Io.

When running, we get this output:

```
$ io actors.io
1122334455
we want the result now
called
after
42
```

You can see the cooperative nature of the actors in how they print their values between each other. You might also notice that the output from the method we called as a future doesn't get called until the last moment.

Another aspect of Io that is very powerful is its support for reflection and metaprogramming; basically, anything is accessible to look at or change. All code in Io is accessible at runtime, represented in the form of messages. You can do many useful things with them, including creating advanced macro facilities. This small example shows you a bit of the power of this approach, even though the specific example might not be that compelling:

```
MostInterestingLanguages/io/meta.io
add := method(n,
  n + 10)

add(40) println

getSlot("add") println
getSlot("add") message println
getSlot("add") message next println
getSlot("add") message next setName("-")

add(40) println
```

First, this code creates a method to add ten to any argument. We call it to see that it works, and then we use getSlot() to get access to the method object without actually evaluating it. We print it and then get the message object inside of it and print that. Messages are chained so that after evaluating one message, Io will follow the next pointer to figure out what to do next. So, we print the next pointer and then change the name of the next message. Finally, we try to add forty again. Basically, this code is changing the implementation of the add() method dynamically, at runtime.

And when we run it, we can see that it works.

```
$ io meta.io
50

# meta.io:2
method(n,
    n + 10
)
n +(10)
+(10)
30
```

Io is extremely malleable. Almost everything is accessible and changeable. It is a very powerful language, and it's powerful by having a very small surface area. It blew my mind when I first learned it, and it continues to blow my mind on a regular basis.

Resources

Io doesn't have any books written about it, but the introduction guide at http://www.iolanguage.com/scm/io/docs/IoGuide.html gives a nice grounding in the language. After you've worked through it, you should be able to look through the reference documentation and understand what's going on. Since Io is also very introspective, you can usually find out what slots an object has by just asking for it.

Steve Dekorte has several talks online about Io, and the book *Seven Languages in Seven Weeks* by Bruce Tate also has a chapter about Io.

2.3 Wrapping Up

If you have any interest in programming languages, this is an interesting time to live in. I've tried to show a few different languages and some of the aspects that make them interesting. From this point on, the responsibility is yours. Go out and discover what's going on. Find other interesting languages and see what you can do in them. One of the effects of learning a new language is that it usually changes how you program in your main programming language too. This transformative effect can be very powerful, especially if you go for a language with a completely different paradigm.

There are many interesting languages that would have been nice to cover in this chapter. However, that would have made the chapter into a book. Some of the languages—both old and new—that I considered covering here are (in no particular order): Frink, Ruby, Scala, Mirah, F#, Prolog, Go, and Self.

I'm writing this on New Year's Eve, and one of the common traditions for this day is that you make yourself a resolution for the next year. Among programmers, choosing and learning a new language is a traditional resolution—started by the Pragmatic Programmers. So, I recommend you do just that. It will make you a better programmer.

CHAPTER 3

Object-Oriented Programming:
Objects over Classes

by Aman King

Some years ago, if you'd asked me for an object-oriented solution, I'd have given you a complete list of classes, with data attributes, method signatures, and a well-structured inheritance hierarchy that you'd readily agree with!

Today, I'll promise to give you only a working system, with multitudes of thriving objects, all working toward solving your problem. I'm willing to state that in most cases, that's all you need.

So, what has changed between then and now?

The first prominent difference is in the way many of us code. Earlier we'd design up front, followed by a close implementation. Today we design as we implement. Focused sessions of test-driven development help us continually evolve code, including external interfaces and internal implementations.

The second major change is in our toolkit of programming languages and frameworks. Earlier it was all Java. Today we spend a year on Ruby using Rails, ActiveRecord, and such, followed by a year of Java projects using Struts 2, Hibernate, and so on. We also work a lot with JavaScript.

These changes have influenced programmers' thoughts about object-oriented programming.

Test-driving our code has taught agile developers to avoid prematurely made, far-reaching design decisions.

Moving between languages has made us take a closer look at common programming paradigms. Java, Ruby, and JavaScript—all OO languages—

have a different spin on fundamental concepts that are sometimes subtle and sometimes dramatic.

This essay is not a treatise on test-driven development, not an elucidation of object-oriented design, and not a language comparison. I'll simply talk about the impacts of an "objects over classes" mind-set on object-oriented programming. Perhaps some of these observations could affect your own design and implementation choices.

3.1   Objects over Classes?

What is a "objects over classes" mind-set?

Well, it's the presiding idea that comes out of thoughts around "objects above classes" in Java, "classes as objects" in Ruby, and "objects in lieu of classes" in JavaScript.

Consider a software solution to a business problem. Irrespective of how you approach it, the solution will ultimately take the form of an application that needs a runtime environment to function. Multiple instructions get executed within this environment, and combinations of these instructions lead to the business problem getting solved.

As a programmer, you need to understand this environment. After all, you're the one who starts off everything, stating what may happen, when it may happen, and how it may happen.

This is where the *object-oriented paradigm* comes in. It gives you a mental model to envision how things take place within the runtime environment. You see the entire system as an ecosystem where various *objects* interact with each other. These objects are entities that tell other entities what to do, react to other entities, change their states, are either introverted or chatty, and are short-lived or sometimes immortal.

Not everyone looks at the runtime environment in the same way: alternate views include paradigms such as procedural, functional, event-driven, and so on. However, the OO paradigm is, by far, the most popular. It is implemented by doing *object-oriented programming* using *object-oriented languages*. These languages provide constructs for specifying object behavior and state.

OO languages can differ in the representational model they allow programmers to use, although there are more commonalities than differences. It's only when you come across a stark distinction that you feel like taking a step back to *think*.

Besides the object, an important concept in OO is the *class*. It's a construct provided by most OO languages to define a template or a blueprint for creating objects.

How do these traditional class constructs help?

At a high level, they allow you to see an unchanging view of the system in one shot, as a network of interconnected classes. They can be connected by inheritance, composition, or collaboration.

At a more focused level, classes represent individual domain concepts, capturing data attributes and operations. Often classes share common properties that are pulled into an inherited generalization. This creates a taxonomy that is observable in the real world.

At a low level, classes define the contract for their instances' interactions, usually accompanied with implementation.

But what's the role of a class in a running application? Once kick-started, almost all heavy lifting is done by objects within the environment. Classes play a passive role, acting only as reference templates for creating new instances. An exception to this is a class with class-level methods that get invoked during runtime.

Classes, as described earlier, play a significant role mostly during an application's conceptualization and construction. As such, I see them as a designing tool for capturing a static representation of the system. They are of limited use during runtime.

Trygve Reenskaug [RWL95], creator of the MVC pattern and contributor to the UML modeling language, once had this to say about the topic:

> *"The class/object duality is essential to both object oriented programming and to object oriented modeling."*

This distinction and the impact of recognizing this duality is what I hope to cover. If we agree that working software matters the most, can't we say that the runtime environment is as important as its static representation? As we design and implement, shouldn't we weigh object-related considerations, in addition to and sometimes over class-related considerations?

3.2 Class Focus vs. Object Focus

Let's begin by differentiating between a class-focused approach and an object-focused approach.

A *class-focused approach* is what I deem to be driven by the goal of modeling the domain in a way the business will recognize it. It does not explicitly track how domain concepts interplay over the course of time but attempts to cover every detail in a single static snapshot. A typical way to come up with a class-based solution is to mark all nouns in a given problem statement and to make classes for each of them. Generalizations and specializations figure their way in as an inheritance hierarchy. A typical example from an enterprise domain will have classes like Person, Employee, Manager, SeniorManager, and so on.

In an *object-focused approach*, the possible runtime relationships and inter-actions of an object become the driving factor behind the design. It leads to representations of the various roles a domain concept can play at different points in time. There may be an overlap of these roles between multiple domain entities. For example, roles in an enterprise domain include Billable, NonBillable, Delegator, Approver, Reportee, and so on.

The Role of Roles

Let's take our example further. In an enterprise, it'd be intuitive to assume that a Senior Manager is a specialization over a Manager, who is an Employee, who obviously is a Person. However, in the runtime environment, let's say on a typical day in office, do you see your Senior Manager *visibly* made up of individual parts, some beaming down from a phantom of an Employee and some from a ghostly Person? That'd be funny if all too apparent. In reality, the Senior Manager is just one complete being, who is performing many important roles. If you need approval of a proposal bid, she'd be the *approver*. If you need to report your timesheet, she'd be your *reporter*. On days when she's on leave, she'd *delegate* such tasks to a Manager who'd easily substitute into the roles of approver and reporter for you.

If the focus isn't on roles, the class structure for the previous domain may look like the following in Java:

```java
class Person {
  // ...
}
class Employee extends Person {
  // ...
}
class Manager extends Employee {
  // ...
}
class SeniorManager extends Manager {
  // ...
}
```

```
class SalesAssociate extends Employee {
  // ...
}
```

If, however, we were to represent roles that the domain entities could play, we might end up with this:

```
interface Approver {
  // ...
}
interface Delegator {
  // ...
}
interface ProposalWriter {
  // ...
}
class SeniorManager implements Approver, Delegator {
  // ...
}
class Manager implements Approver {
  // ...
}
class SalesAssociate implements ProposalWriter {
  // ...
}
```

Notice how every role is represented by a *role interface.*[1] All the domain entity classes like SeniorManager, Manager, and so on, implement these roles as appropriate. Also note the complete lack of inheritance. So, how is code reused? Surely there must be similarities between how a Senior Manager or a Manager performs approvals.

In the runtime environment, where inheritance doesn't play a *visible* role, inheritance is reduced to a technique for reusing code and avoiding duplication. But there are other ways of achieving reuse, one being composition with delegation. So, perhaps composition may be an alternative to inheritance.[2] Let's see how.

```
interface Approver {
  ApprovalDecision decideApproval(ApprovalRequest approvalRequest);
}
class MediumLevelApprovalStrategy implements Approver {
  public ApprovalDecision decideApproval(ApprovalRequest approvalRequest) {
    // ... some business decision rules
    return approvalDecision;
  }
```

---

1. http://martinfowler.com/bliki/RoleInterface.html
2. http://c2.com/cgi/wiki?DelegationIsInheritance

```
}
class LowLevelApprovalStrategy implements Approver {
  // ...
}
class SeniorManager implements Approver, Delegator {
  Approver approvalStrategy = new MediumLevelApprovalStrategy();
  public SeniorManager(String name) {
    // ...
  }
  public ApprovalDecision decideApproval(ApprovalRequest approvalRequest) {
    return approvalStrategy.decideApproval(approvalRequest);
  }
  // ...
}
class Manager implements Approver {
  Approver approvalStrategy = new LowLevelApprovalStrategy();
  public Manager(String name) {
    // ...
  }
  public ApprovalDecision decideApproval(ApprovalRequest approvalRequest) {
    return approvalStrategy.decideApproval(approvalRequest);
  }
  // ...
}
```

As seen, the domain entities instantiate a strategy of their choice and then trust it to do the decision making for them. In this case, the Manager uses a low-level approval strategy, while the Senior Manager uses a medium-level strategy. This approach makes everything very explicit and gets away from complexities of selective method overrides, template methods, private vs. protected access, and so on, which are all part and parcel of complex inheritance structures.

An added benefit is that the reuse happens at runtime. It is trivial to change existing dependencies as the live situation changes. For example, the Senior Manager based on certain conditions could change her approval strategy to be low level for some time, only to later go back to a medium-level strategy. This can't be easily achieved with inheritance where the implementation is locked down at compile time.

Now let's consider another example: the problem statement is of generating a voter list. Voters can be people who are 18 years or older and who are nationals of a certain country. To introduce complexity, we'll state that voters can also be countries that can vote within councils of nations that they're members of. Given the domain entities, we can have classes like these:

ObjectsOverClasses/java/voterlist/classbased/VoterListClassBased.java

```java
class CouncilOfNations {
    private Collection<Country> memberNations;
    public CouncilOfNations(Collection<Country> memberNations) {
        this.memberNations = memberNations;
    }
    public boolean contains(Country country) {
        return memberNations.contains(country);
    }
}

class Country {
    private String name;
    public Country(String name) {
        this.name = name;
    }
}

class Person {
    private String name;
    private int age;
    private Country country;
    public Person(String name, int age, Country country) {
        // ...
    }
    public boolean canVoteIn(Country votingJurisdiction) {
        return age >= 18 && votingJurisdiction.equals(country);
    }
}

abstract class AbstractVoterList<T, X> {
    private Collection<T> candidateVoters;
    public AbstractVoterList(Collection<T> candidateVoters) {
        this.candidateVoters = candidateVoters;
    }
    public Collection<T> votersFor(X votingJurisdiction) {
        Collection<T> eligibleVoters = new HashSet<T>();
        for (T voter : candidateVoters) {
            if (canVoteIn(voter, votingJurisdiction)) {
                eligibleVoters.add(voter);
            }
        }
        return eligibleVoters;
    }
    protected abstract boolean canVoteIn(T voter, X votingJurisdiction);
}
class PersonVoterList extends AbstractVoterList<Person, Country> {
    public PersonVoterList(Collection<Person> persons) {
        super(persons);
    }
```

```java
    protected boolean canVoteIn(Person person, Country country) {
        return person.canVoteIn(country);
    }
}
class CountryVoterList extends AbstractVoterList<Country, CouncilOfNations> {
    public CountryVoterList(Collection<Country> countries) {
        super(countries);
    }
    protected boolean canVoteIn(Country country,
                                CouncilOfNations councilOfNations) {
        return councilOfNations.contains(country);
    }
}
```

The previous can be invoked like this:

ObjectsOverClasses/java/voterlist/classbased/VoterListClassBased.java

```java
Country INDIA = new Country("India");
Country USA = new Country("USA");
Country UK = new Country("UK");
Collection<Person> persons = asList(
    new Person("Donald", 28, INDIA),
    new Person("Daisy", 25, USA),
    new Person("Minnie", 17, UK)
);
PersonVoterList personVoterList = new PersonVoterList(persons);
System.out.println(personVoterList.votersFor(INDIA)); // [ Donald ]
System.out.println(personVoterList.votersFor(USA));   // [ Daisy ]
Collection<Country> countries = asList(INDIA, USA, UK);
CountryVoterList countryVoterList = new CountryVoterList(countries);
CouncilOfNations councilOfNations = new CouncilOfNations(asList(
    USA, INDIA
));
System.out.println(countryVoterList.votersFor(councilOfNations));
// [ USA, India ]
```

If we were to convert the previous into a more object-focused solution, we need to start by looking at important interaction points and come up with new names for the collaborators according to what they're doing, rather than what they are. Once identified, we can use refactorings like *Extract Interface*, *Pull Up Method*, and *Rename Method* to change the code structure to look something like this:

ObjectsOverClasses/java/voterlist/rolebased/VoterListRoleBased.java

```java
interface VotingJurisdiction {
    boolean covers(VotingJurisdiction votingJurisdiction);
}
interface Voter {
    boolean canVoteIn(VotingJurisdiction votingJurisdiction);
}
```

```
class CouncilOfNations implements VotingJurisdiction {
    private Collection<Country> memberNations;
    public CouncilOfNations(Collection<Country> memberNations) {
        this.memberNations = memberNations;
    }
    public boolean covers(VotingJurisdiction votingJurisdiction) {
        return this.equals(votingJurisdiction) ||
            memberNations.contains(votingJurisdiction);
    }
}
class Country implements VotingJurisdiction, Voter {
    private String name;
    public Country(String name) {
        this.name = name;
    }
    public boolean covers(VotingJurisdiction votingJurisdiction) {
        return this.equals(votingJurisdiction);
    }
    public boolean canVoteIn(VotingJurisdiction votingJurisdiction) {
        return votingJurisdiction.covers(this);
    }
}
class Person implements Voter {
    private String name;
    private int age;
    private Country country;
    public Person(String name, int age, Country country) {
        // ...
    }
    public boolean canVoteIn(VotingJurisdiction votingJurisdiction) {
        return age >= 18 && votingJurisdiction.covers(country);
    }
}
class VoterList {
    private Collection<Voter> candidateVoters;
    public VoterList(Collection<Voter> candidateVoters) {
        this.candidateVoters = candidateVoters;
    }
    public Collection<Voter> votersFor(VotingJurisdiction votingJurisdiction) {
        Collection<Voter> eligibleVoters = new HashSet<Voter>();
        for (Voter voter : candidateVoters) {
            if (voter.canVoteIn(votingJurisdiction)) {
                eligibleVoters.add(voter);
            }
        }
        return eligibleVoters;
    }
}
```

The usage remains very similar to the previous case, except that both person-VoterList and countryVoterList will be instances of the same class: VoterList.

The former solution effectively uses inheritance combined with generics and the template method design pattern. The latter solution is implemented using role interfaces, which ends up needing neither generics nor any apparent design pattern.

There are further differences between the two solutions.

In the first approach, PersonVoterList allows only for checking a Person instance against a Country jurisdiction, and CountryVoterList checks only between a Country and a CouncilOfNations.

In the second approach, VoterList can check any kind of Voter implementation against any kind of VotingJurisdiction implementation. For example, personVoterList.votersFor(councilOfNations) returns a consolidated list of [Donald, Daisy] across the countries [INDIA, USA].

The philosophy behind the latter approach is that when it comes to interactions, what matters is not what *type* of object an argument is (as in Person, Country, or CouncilOfNations) but whether the object can play an expected role or not (like Voter and VotingJurisdiction).

The former approach creates a restrictive system where an object is highly constrained in its choices of what other objects it can interact with. With role interfaces, an object can be more *promiscuous* with respect to collaboration. Objects will be expecting only subsets of interfaces to be satisfied at a time, allowing many different types of objects to satisfy these minimal interfaces. Determining whether the interaction itself makes sense is left to the consuming code, which can be validated by unit tests.

With an object-focused mind-set, you should be thinking more in terms of role interfaces as opposed to header interfaces. A *header interface*[3] helps only in specifying a complete contract for a class. It discourages the notion of instances taking on any behavior not covered by the interface. It also places strict demands on substitute implementations that will need to satisfy the complete interface or nothing at all.

Header interfaces are prevalent in projects where programmers make a habit out of what Martin Fowler describes as "the practice of taking every class and pairing it with an interface."[4]

---

3. http://martinfowler.com/bliki/HeaderInterface.html
4. http://martinfowler.com/bliki/InterfaceImplementationPair.html

Separation of Responsibilities

Another aspect to object focus is actively thinking about responsibilities that belong to a class vs. those of an object. Remember that in a live environment, objects are more active than classes. You should enhance these objects where possible instead of introducing class-level behavior. The question to ask is, "Should a class really be doing more than defining behavior of its instances?"

The following code is a *utility class*, something that quickly crops up in almost any project. These classes defy the expectation of acting as a blueprint and participate during runtime directly. They are usually stateless and hold multiple class-level *helper methods* that apply transformations on a set of inputs to return a desired output. These methods seem more procedural than OO.

As a project progresses, utility classes tend to bloat, sometimes to a scary extent! They can end up with all kinds of logic, ranging from seemingly harmless wrapper methods around primitive data types to critical domain-specific business rules. Bringing a rampant utility class back under control can be difficult. So, what can we do about functionality such as the following?

ObjectsOverClasses/java/utility/Utils.java
```java
public class Utils {
    // ...
    public static String capitalize(String value) {
        if (value.length() == 0) return "";
        return value.substring(0, 1).toUpperCase() + value.substring(1);
    }
    // ...
    private static String join(List<? extends Object> values,
                               String delimiter) {
        String result = "";
        // ...
        return result;
    }
}
```

We can split these behaviors into individual classes with instance-level methods. Instances of core classes can then be decorated by these new wrapper classes.

ObjectsOverClasses/java/utility/Extensions.java
```java
class ExtendedString {
    private String value;
    public ExtendedString(String value) {
        this.value = value;
    }
```

```java
    public String toString() {
        return value;
    }
    public ExtendedString capitalize() {
        if (value.length() == 0) return new ExtendedString("");
        return new ExtendedString(
            value.substring(0, 1).toUpperCase() + value.substring(1)
        );
    }
}
class ExtendedList<T> extends ArrayList<T> {
    public ExtendedList(List<T> list) {
        super(list);
    }

    public String join(String delimiter) {
        String result = "";
        // ...
        return result;
    }
}
```

Here's the difference in the usages:

ObjectsOverClasses/java/utility/Utils.java
```java
String name = Utils.capitalize("king"); // "King"

List<String> list = asList("hello", "world");
String joinedList = Utils.join(list, ", "); // "hello, world"
```

ObjectsOverClasses/java/utility/Extensions.java
```java
ExtendedString extendedString = new ExtendedString("king");
String name = extendedString.capitalize().toString(); // "King"

ExtendedList<String> extendedList =
    new ExtendedList<String>(asList("hello", "world"));
String joinedList = extendedList.join(", "); // "hello, world"
```

Notice that in the former case, the functionality is globally accessible across the code base by virtue of being associated with a class. In the latter case, the functionality is available only if the consuming code has access to the right objects. This distinction is reminiscent of the global variables of yesteryear. There are similar risks[5] with class-level methods, especially if they modify class-level state.

I first came across the technique of decorating instances at runtime in Martin Fowler's *Refactoring [FBBO99]* book as a refactoring named *Introduce Local*

---

5. http://c2.com/cgi/wiki?GlobalVariablesAreBad

Extension. It's useful when you can't add behavior to a class directly because you don't have control over it, like Java's String.

With core data types such as integers, strings, and arrays, the problem may not remain restricted to class-level methods. If objects freely accept primitives as method parameters or are composed of the same, the objects may end up with misplaced responsibilities. A classic example in Java is using Double to represent money or using String for ZIP codes, telephone numbers, and email addresses. In most projects, such fields will be accompanied by special formatting or validation requirements. This is when we may struggle to find a place for corresponding logic. If the code doesn't end up in a utility class, it's likely to land in the object dealing with the primitive value. Neither is ideal. The *Refactoring [FBBO99]* book lists this *code smell* as *Primitive Obsession* and suggests refactorings like *Replace Data Value with Object* and *Replace Type Code with Class.*

Java's Calendar API is a real-world example of having numerous methods that accept and return primitive number values. Because of the resulting unwieldy API, Joda Time, a cleaner and more object-oriented alternative, has gained much popularity.[6]

Testing Perspective

There are two sides to testing with respect to an object focus.

On the one hand, test-driving your code, while having scenarios in mind instead of classes, can push you toward designs that are object-focused rather than class-focused. Since you're dealing with only one interaction at a time, you think about the roles of the objects in question rather than entire domain concepts. This may drive you to build your domain modeling gradually, evolving role after role. You may be surprised to see how many different domain entities suddenly fit into the roles you identify, which is something you may not catch otherwise.

On the other hand, if your solution has an object-focused design, its testability improves further. Techniques such as role interfaces make it especially easy to test collaborations . You may use a mocking framework, but trivially created stubs can suffice. Avoiding class-level methods further allows consuming code to invoke behavior via collaborators that are dependency-injectable, not hardwired. This makes mock substitutions possible.

---

6. http://joda-time.sourceforge.net

Here's how you can use stubs to unit test the role-based VoterList without needing to involve either Person or Country:

```
ObjectsOverClasses/java/voterlist/rolebased/VoterListTest.java
public class VoterListTest {
    @Test
    public void shouldSelectThoseWhoCanVote() {
        Voter eligibleVoter1 = new VoterWithEligibility(true);
        Voter eligibleVoter2 = new VoterWithEligibility(true);
        Voter ineligibleVoter = new VoterWithEligibility(false);
        Collection<Voter> candidateVoters = new HashSet<Voter>(asList(
            eligibleVoter1, ineligibleVoter, eligibleVoter2
        ));
        Collection<Voter> expectedVoters = new HashSet<Voter>(asList(
            eligibleVoter1, eligibleVoter2
        ));
        VoterList voterList = new VoterList(candidateVoters);
        assertEquals(expectedVoters,
            voterList.votersFor(new AnyVotingJurisdiction()));
    }

    static class VoterWithEligibility implements Voter {
        private boolean eligibility;
        public VoterWithEligibility(boolean eligibility) {
            this.eligibility = eligibility;
        }
        public boolean canVoteIn(VotingJurisdiction votingJurisdiction) {
            return eligibility;
        }
    }
    static class AnyVotingJurisdiction implements VotingJurisdiction {
        public boolean covers(VotingJurisdiction votingJurisdiction) {
            return true;
        }
    }
}
```

Steve Freeman, Nat Pryce, et al., share further thoughts on test-driving roles in their OOPSLA paper, *Mock Roles, Not Objects [FPMW04]*.

Code Base Indicators

Now that you've seen examples of class-focused solutions along with object-focused counterparts, will you be able to spot them in your own project? I'll share some signs that could help.

Do you use a framework that requires inheritance to work? A subclass is restricted in what it can reuse via inheritance. There are also constraints applied to its constructors. Such compile-time restrictions on the evolution of a class indicate a lack of object-based thinking. Try to use framework-coupled classes only for plugging into the framework. Keep domain logic in separate classes that can change independently.

Do you have classes three or four levels deep in their inheritance hierarchy? Having multiple levels of inheritance means more and more behavior is accumulated at every level, leading to heavy objects that can do too many things. Question how much of the inherited behavior is actually relevant as per usage. Heavy objects are also difficult to unit test in isolation because they're hardwired to parent implementations. Even a *test-specific subclass*[7] will be cumbersome if you need to override multiple methods for stubbing.

Do you have more classes than you care for, especially those with only minor variations? Class explosion can be a sign of class-based thinking. Deep inheritance hierarchies result in too many classes. This worsens if parallel hierarchies exist. As an example, for every subclass of Car, say Sedan and Hatchback, we may need a corresponding Chassis, like SedanChassis and HatchbackChassis. At this point, we need to identify common roles across the classes and try composition instead of inheritance.

Do you have too few classes, each of them rather bloated? A system is healthy if there are multiple objects talking to each other, not if only a few introverted objects perform all the tasks. Having few classes indicates that responsibilities are distributed only among some objects during runtime. On top of that, if class-level methods are prevalent, classes are owning tasks that would otherwise be performed by objects. Note that having small independent classes as blueprints of objects with single responsibilities is different from having many deceptively small classes that inherit shared behavior and vary only marginally. The former is a positive sign of loose coupling, while the latter reflects high coupling.

There can be more of such indicators, but this list is a good starting point. Regular code introspection can be useful for a project: I've been part of teams that made it a practice, and it helped improve the quality of our code base.

3.3 Object-Focused Languages

So far, I've talked about the impact of object thinking, giving importance to "objects above classes." The ideas were language independent, even though I used Java for example code. We'll now shift focus to OO languages that stand out with respect to their treatment of objects. Unlike conventional languages such as Java and C#, they support object-focused design and

---

7.   http://xunitpatterns.com/Test-Specific%20Subclass.html

implementation in natural, idiomatic ways. It is easier to realize object thinking when you play to a language's strengths rather than work around them.

I'll start with Ruby and JavaScript, both languages more than fifteen years old but that have seen renewed interest of late. I'll wrap up by briefly touching upon Groovy and Scala, comparatively younger languages.

Ruby

Ruby has brought to the forefront the idea of objects as a central character. Its most powerful feature is that everything is an object,[8] especially its treatment of *classes as objects.*

ObjectsOverClasses/ruby/objects.rb
```ruby
class Greeter
  def hi
    'hi'
  end
end
puts Greeter.new.kind_of? Object                   #=> true, an instance is an object
puts Greeter.kind_of? Object                       #=> true, a class is an object
puts Greeter.new.method(:hi).kind_of? Object #=> true, a method is an object
puts proc { puts 'hello' }.kind_of? Object    #=> true, a code block is an object
puts 1.kind_of? Object                             #=> true, core data types are objects
puts 'a'.kind_of? Object                           #=> true, core data types are objects
puts :some_symbol.kind_of? Object                  #=> true, core data types are objects
puts [1,2,3].kind_of? Object                       #=> true, core data types are objects
puts ({:a => 'a'}).kind_of? Object                 #=> true, core data types are objects
```

Let's look at another syntax that could define the Greeter class.

```ruby
Greeter = Class.new do
  def hi
    'hi'
  end
end
```

The previous highlights that Greeter is a global constant, referencing an instance of the class Class. It was created by an invocation of new() on Class, with a code block argument that represented the new class's definition. The Greeter class object itself has useful methods such as the following:

new()   Creates a new instance of the class, initializing it as needed.

methods()   Returns a list of methods that can be invoked on the class object itself.

---

8. Code blocks are not converted into objects until required.

instance_methods()	Returns a list of methods that can be invoked on the class's instance.
ancestors()	Returns a list of participants in the class's ancestry, starting with the class itself and then moving up the inheritance chain.
class_eval()	Takes a code block or a string as an argument and then evaluates it as Ruby code within its own context. This method is key to metaprogramming in Ruby.

Ruby treats a class as a container of behavior rather than as a frozen template or a strong data type. With a class being an object and a container, it's only natural to think that you can get hold of it during runtime and add more behavior into it. Here's a demonstration of how easy it is to do just that! Note that Greeter doesn't start off with the instance methods hello() and goodbye(); we define them dynamically.

ObjectsOverClasses/ruby/metaprogramming.rb

```ruby
['hello', 'goodbye'].each do |greeting|
  Greeter.class_eval <<-MULTILINE_STRING
    def #{greeting}(name)
      "#{greeting} \#{name}!"
    end
  MULTILINE_STRING
end
greeter = Greeter.new
puts greeter.hello('Aman') #=> hello Aman!
puts greeter.goodbye('King') #=> goodbye King!
```

Metaprogramming is not the only way to add behavior to an existing class. In Ruby, a class is *open*, meaning its definition is not closed-ended or a one-time specification; it can be amended during runtime. This includes core Ruby classes.

ObjectsOverClasses/ruby/extensions.rb

```ruby
class String # reopening core String class
  def custom_capitalize
    "#{self[0,1].upcase}#{self[1..-1]}"
  end
end
class Array # reopening core Array class
  def custom_join(delimiter)
    # ...
  end
end
puts "king".custom_capitalize #=> King
puts ['hello', 'world'].custom_join(', ') #=> hello, world
```

The Ruby runtime ensures that any instance of a class can be used to invoke any of the class's instance methods, irrespective of how and when those methods were defined. This works because when a method is called on an object, it is treated as a *message*, having a name and a list of arguments. For each invocation, Ruby dynamically passes this message to participants in the object's lookup chain, from bottom to top, until one of them accepts and processes the message. If none responds, a special method called method_missing() is called on the object, passing it the message details. This method raises a NoMethodError by default but can be overridden to achieve interesting results.

An object's lookup chain can have the following kinds of participants:

Class   This is a class object that participates in the inheritance hierarchy of the object. Its position, relative to other classes, follows the order of inheritance between parent and child classes. The class at the bottom will be the object's immediate class, and the class at the top will be BasicObject.[9]

Module   A module can represent a *mixin*[10] in Ruby. It is essentially a collection of behavior that can be included in a class, without it being part of the explicit inheritance hierarchy. It's added in the lookup chain above the class that includes it.

Eigen class   This is an anonymous hidden class that holds instance methods very specific to the object itself, such that these instance methods, aka *singleton methods*, are invokable only on that particular object and not on any other. The eigen class is created only when needed and takes its position at the very bottom of the lookup chain, even below the object's actual class.

The following is a demonstration of the previously mentioned singleton methods, yet another language feature that treats objects as first-class citizens; an object can have methods exclusive to it!

ObjectsOverClasses/ruby/singleton_methods.rb

```ruby
class Person
  # empty class
end
peter = Person.new
def peter.crawl_walls # define singleton method on peter
  "Look, Ma! I can crawl walls!"
end
```

---

9.   Prior to Ruby 1.9, Object was the parent of all classes.

10. http://c2.com/cgi/wiki?MixIn

```
puts peter.crawl_walls #=> Look, Ma! I can crawl walls!
aman = Person.new
puts aman.crawl_walls # NoMethodError: undefined method 'crawl_walls'
```

Given that a class may be metaprogrammed, be opened multiple times, or have behavior mixed in, or that objects can have singleton methods, it suffices to say that contracts are only loosely defined in Ruby. This holds true for method parameters too: they don't have any data type constraints. Any object may be passed as any parameter. The method should typically just assume that the passed object satisfies the necessary contract. That said, to query for a specific contract, respond_to? can be used.

ObjectsOverClasses/ruby/duck_typing.rb
```
class Spider
  def crawl_walls
    "crawling..."
  end
end
class Person
  # empty class
end
def make_crawl(obj) # no type constraints on obj
  if obj.respond_to? :crawl_walls
    puts obj.crawl_walls
  else
    puts "cannot crawl walls"
  end
end

peter = Person.new
def peter.crawl_walls
  "Look, Ma! I can crawl walls!"
end
make_crawl(Spider.new) #=> crawling...
make_crawl(Person.new) #=> cannot crawl walls
make_crawl(peter) #=> Look, Ma! I can crawl walls!
```

Such dynamic typing is called *duck typing*:

> *"When I see a bird that walks like a duck and swims like a duck and quacks like a duck, I call that bird a duck."*[11]

We earlier talked about role interfaces, which focus more on the collaboration at hand than defining a complete contract for objects. Duck typing makes these roles implicit. Some people may have reservations around type safety. But high unit test coverage is expected to ensure only valid interactions occur, and this is well supported by the practice of test-driven development. There

---

11. Quote attributed to James Whitcomb Riley: http://en.wikipedia.org/wiki/Duck_typing

is still a risk, but Rubyists generally accept the trade-off for more freedom. Having been part of many Ruby projects, I can affirm that it's a profitable trade-off indeed!

We'll now see how you could use Ruby's language features on your own project. The examples are derivations of general patterns I've seen in the projects I've been part of.

Every now and then, programmers run into a need for a data transfer object. A typical characteristic of these objects is that they need field-based equality and accessor methods. At one point in a project, we had classes like the following being populated from XML feeds:

```ruby
ObjectsOverClasses/ruby/blog_example.rb
class BlogPost
  attr_reader :title, :updated_at, :content
  def initialize(params)
    @title = params[:title]
    @updated_at = params[:updated_at]
    @content = params[:content]
  end
  def current_month?
    today = Time.now
    @updated_at.year == today.year && @updated_at.month == today.month
  end
  def truncated_content(word_limit = 100)
    # ...
  end
  def eql?(other)
    return true if equal?(other)
    @title == other.title && @updated_at == other.updated_at &&
      @content == other.content
  end
  alias_method :==, :eql?
  def hash
    @title.hash + @updated_at.hash + @content.hash
  end
end

class BlogAuthor
  attr_reader :name, :email
  def initialize(params)
    @name = params[:name]
    @email = params[:email]
  end
  def anonymous?
    @name.empty? && @email.empty?
  end
```

```ruby
  def display
    return 'Unknown' if anonymous?
    @name || @email
  end
  def eql?(other)
    return true if equal?(other)
    @name == other.name && @email == other.email
  end
  alias_method :==, :eql?
  def hash
    @name.hash + @email.hash
  end
end
```

At first look, the classes seem distinct and without duplication. But think of code itself as something manipulatable at runtime, and you will notice refactoring opportunities. Recognize that the uninteresting methods, namely, the constructor, the getter methods, the hash code generator, and the equality implementation, are similar between the two classes, except for the attributes used.

If you encounter such code, feel free to tackle it head on, arriving at something like this:

ObjectsOverClasses/ruby/blog_example_cleanup.rb
```ruby
class BlogPost
  include AttributeDriven
  attributes :title, :updated_at, :content # boiler plate generated

  def current_month?
    today = Time.now
    @updated_at.year == today.year && @updated_at.month == today.month
  end
  def truncated_content(word_limit = 100)
    # ...
  end
end

class BlogAuthor
  include AttributeDriven
  attributes :name, :email # boiler plate generated

  def anonymous?
    @name.empty? && @email.empty?
  end
  def display
    return 'Unknown' if anonymous?
    @name || @email
  end
end
```

It's not difficult to write such code, including the *magic* done by AttributeDriven. Behind it is simple metaprogramming that we've already seen. Yet look at the effect of it!

Boilerplate code, which distracts from highlighting domain responsibilities, should be tucked away in other parts of code that simply generate more code. Besides readability, another benefit is that creating new classes with similar boilerplate becomes trivial, both time-wise and effort-wise. This approach doesn't take away from testability or traceability, because each part can be tested for what it does: the domain classes for business logic, the metaprogramming parts for code generation. The Ruby language and its frameworks acknowledge this and support such techniques out of the box. For example, instead of coming up with AttributeDriven as shown earlier, similar cleanup can be achieved using Ruby's built-in Struct class.[12]

It's not always that a class has to be manipulated for readability's sake or for removing boilerplate. Sometimes it becomes necessary to fix bugs or to extend the functionality of a third-party library. We already saw how local extensions help when you don't have control over a third-party class, like Java's String. But with Ruby, as long as a class is accessible within the runtime, the class object behind it can be used to extend its functionality on the fly!

On one of our Ruby-based web projects, we were using a tool suite of Cucumber plus Capybara plus Selenium to automate our functional tests. Over time, our test run duration grew to an undesirable extent. We decided to run individual tests in parallel to reduce the duration. This helped a great deal, but because there were parallel processes using parallel browser instances, Selenium became flaky in talking to browsers, failing tests when it couldn't make a connection in time.

The fix was simple: have Selenium retry a couple of times before giving up. The more interesting part, however, was how we *monkey-patched* this functionality onto an existing library class.

```
require 'retry-this'

module CapybaraParallelizationFix
  def self.included(base)
    base.class_eval {alias_method_chain :visit, :retry} # metaprogramming
  end

  def visit_with_retry(url)
    RetryThis.retry_this(:times => 2) do # reattempt if error occurs
```

---

12. http://www.ruby-doc.org/core/classes/Struct.html

```
        visit_without_retry url # open url in browser
    end
  end
end
# monkey patch the fix onto the Selenium driver
Capybara::Driver::Selenium.send :include, CapybaraParallelizationFix
```

My hope is that the previous examples hint at what kind of programming is possible with Ruby. A lot of this shouldn't be new to developers who work with Ruby on Rails, a popular web framework that encourages readable, fluent APIs. Some parts of the framework implementation are worth a look,[13] and with an understanding of how Ruby treats objects and classes, it should be possible to write similar, clean APIs in our day-to-day programming too.

JavaScript

JavaScript, as an object-oriented language, is rather intriguing—largely because it doesn't have the notion of a class! It follows a paradigm of using *objects in lieu of classes*.

You don't need a class to create an object in JavaScript. An object is simply a collection of properties. The property can be a number, a string, another object, or even a function. JavaScript doesn't distinguish between an object's data fields and its methods.

ObjectsOverClasses/javascript/properties.js
```
var donald = { name: 'Donald', age: 28,
    canVote: function() { return this.age >= 18; } };
for (property in donald) { // iterating over 'name', 'age', 'canVote'
    console.log(donald[property]); // like donald.name, donald.age, etc
}
console.log(donald.name); // Donald
console.log(donald.age); // 28
console.log(donald.canVote); // a function reference
console.log(donald.canVote()); // true, result of invoking the function
```

A *constructor function* can be used to initialize an object. The function itself is not special. If invoked after the keyword new, JavaScript sets the special pointer this within the function to point to a newly created empty object. Any property set on this will be set on that object.

ObjectsOverClasses/javascript/constructorFunction.js
```
function Person(name, age) { // capitalized function name by convention
    this.name = name;
    this.age = age;
}
```

---

13. http://github.com/rails/rails

```
var daisy = new Person('Daisy', 25);
console.log(daisy.name); // Daisy
console.log(daisy.age); // 25
console.log(daisy.constructor == Person); // true
```

Every function in JavaScript is an object. It has a property prototype, pointing to an empty object by default. Custom properties can be bound to the prototype. Objects created by a constructor function will have a link to the function's prototype. Any property accessed on such objects is looked up in the prototype if not found in the object itself. This feature is used to share common properties across all objects created via a particular constructor function. An advantage is that new properties added to a prototype are accessible through existing objects too.

ObjectsOverClasses/javascript/prototypeBasedProgramming.js

```
function Person(name, age) {
    this.name = name;
    this.age = age;
}
Person.prototype.sayHello = function() {
    return this.name + ' says, "Hello!"';
};
var daisy = new Person('Daisy', 25);
console.log(daisy.sayHello()); // Daisy says, "Hello!"
Person.prototype.sayHelloTo = function(another) {
    return this.name + ' says, "Hello, ' + another.name + '!"';
};
var donald = new Person('Donald', 28);
console.log(donald.sayHelloTo(daisy)); // Donald says, "Hello, Daisy!"
console.log(daisy.sayHelloTo(donald)); // Daisy says, "Hello, Donald!"
```

This is *prototype-based programming*: behavior is defined against a well-known object, and other objects are created with a reference to the object.

JavaScript uses this same approach for built-in constructor functions like String() and Array(). This allows us to tack on functionality when needed.

ObjectsOverClasses/javascript/extensions.js

```
String.prototype.capitalize = function() {
    if (this.length == 0) return "";
    return this[0].toUpperCase() + this.substring(1);
};
Array.prototype.customJoin = function(delimiter) {
    var result = '';
    // ...
    return result;
};
console.log("king".capitalize()); // King
console.log(["hello", "world"].customJoin(", ")); // hello, world
```

JavaScript sees extensive usage of its language features across many popular libraries and frameworks. Prototype and jQuery are good examples of such libraries. They provide simple APIs to programmers without introducing complex abstraction layers or hierarchies. They also allow programmers to introduce their own extensions in a uniform way.

The following is a simple usage of jQuery to read and update CSS properties of a DOM object:

```html
<html>
<head>
    <script src="http://code.jquery.com/jquery-1.7.2.js"></script>
    <style>
        div { width:50px; }
    </style>
</head>
<body>
    <div id="content" style="height:100px;">some text</div>
    <script>
        jQuery(function() {
            var contentDiv = jQuery("#content");
            var borderWidth = (parseInt(contentDiv.css("width")) +
                    parseInt(contentDiv.css("height"))) / 10;
            contentDiv.css("border-width", borderWidth)
                .css("border-style", "groove")
                .css("background-color", "yellow");
        });
    </script>
</body>
</html>
```

jQuery uses prototype-based programming to provide clean APIs like jQuery("#content").css("border-width", 15).css("border-style", "groove"). All jQuery objects share a common prototype object, referenced by jQuery.fn. The library adds most of its functionality via this object. Other programmers are encouraged to use the same. The idea is to be consistent in how we interact with jQuery objects, whether for core APIs or our own.

Here's a custom jQuery extension for a max() method on collections:

```
ObjectsOverClasses/javascript/max.js
var personsArray = [ { name: 'Donald', age: 28 }, { name: 'Daisy', age: 25 },
        { name: 'Minnie', age: 17 } ]; // core JS
var persons = jQuery(personsArray); // jQuery wrapper
persons.each(function(index, person) { // jQuery's each
    console.log(person.name);
}); // prints Donald, Daisy, Minnie

jQuery.fn.max = function(customMaxOn) { // custom max method
```

```javascript
    var defaultMaxOn = (function(element) { return element; });
    var maxOn = customMaxOn || defaultMaxOn;
    var max;
    jQuery(this).each(function(index, element) {
        if (!max || maxOn(max) <= maxOn(element)) {
            max = element;
        }
    });
    return max;
};
console.log( persons.max(function(person) { return person.name; }) );
// { name: 'Minnie', age: 17 }
console.log( persons.max(function(person) { return person.age; }) );
// { name: 'Donald', age: 28 }
```

Studying the JavaScript programming model can be useful, for both academic value and practical usage. This is especially true with many contemporary websites relying heavily on it and rich UI libraries like Ext JS emerging strongly. JavaScript is also moving beyond web browsers, such as the use of Node.js for server-side network programming.

Groovy

Groovy is an OO language designed to run on the Java Virtual Machine. It draws similarities with Ruby and shares certain features such as duck typing. Some of its language features make objects quite useful, especially when integrating with Java.

In Groovy, a *metaclass* serves as an interface point to an object. The Groovy runtime uses it for property and method access. Normal Groovy objects use it for metaprogramming. ExpandoMetaClass is a metaclass implementation that allows manipulating methods and properties on the fly. Here's an example from the Groovy docs:[14]

ObjectsOverClasses/groovy/metaClass.groovy
```groovy
class Student {
    List schedule = []
    def addLecture(String lecture) { schedule << lecture }
}
class Worker {
    List schedule = []
    def addMeeting(String meeting) { schedule << meeting }
}
def collegeStudent = new Object()
collegeStudent.metaClass {
    mixin Student, Worker
```

---

14. http://groovy.codehaus.org/api/groovy/lang/ExpandoMetaClass.html

```
    getSchedule {
        mixedIn[Student].schedule + mixedIn[Worker].schedule
    }
}
collegeStudent.with {
    addMeeting('Performance review with Boss')
    addLecture('Learn about Groovy Mixins')
    println schedule
    // [Learn about Groovy Mixins, Performance review with Boss]
}
```

Observe how collegeStudent acquires the behavior of Student and Worker because of mixins on the object's metaClass.

Java interfaces can be implemented within Groovy. Like duck typing, any object can stand in for a Java interface. Any method that the object doesn't implement will result in a runtime exception upon invocation, but Java will still accept the object as the specified interface's implementation. Following is an example of Groovy maps implementing Java interfaces of Iterator and Transformer:[15]

ObjectsOverClasses/groovy/interfaceImplementations.groovy

```
import org.apache.commons.collections.*

impl = [
    i: 10,
    hasNext: { impl.i > 0 },
    next: { impl.i-- }
]
iterator = impl as Iterator
toSquare = [ transform: {e -> e * e} ] as Transformer
println CollectionUtils.collect(iterator, toSquare)
// [100, 81, 64, 49, 36, 25, 16, 9, 4, 1]
```

Scala

Scala is a statically typed language that runs on the Java Virtual Machine. *Programming in Scala [OSV08]* mentions that the language benefits from an advanced static type system, complemented by a type inference mechanism. Despite being type-focused, some Scala features give due importance to objects. For starters, every *value* is an object in Scala, and operators are method invocations on objects.

Perhaps more fundamental is that there is no static keyword in Scala: the language doesn't entertain members at a class level. This prevents a class from having responsibilities other than defining a template for instances. In

---

15. http://groovy.codehaus.org/Groovy+way+to+implement+interfaces

lieu of using static, programmers sometimes use Scala's *singleton object* feature. A singleton object is instantiated by Scala automatically, and there is only one instance of it, following the singleton pattern. A singleton object and a class can coexist with the same name.

```scala
ObjectsOverClasses/scala/singleton-objects.scala
class Person(val id:Int, val name:String, val age:Int) {
  def canVote() = { age >= 18 }
}
object Person { // singleton object
  private val persons = List(new Person(1, "Donald", 28),
    new Person(2, "Daisy", 25), new Person(3, "Minnie", 17))
  def findById(id:Int):Person = {
    persons.find(person => person.id == id).get
  }
  def findAllByName(name:String):List[Person] = {
    persons.filter(person => person.name == name)
  }
}
var person = Person.findById(2)
println(person.name + " can vote: " + person.canVote())
// Daisy can vote: true
```

I hope this section highlighted how different languages have different takes on the same paradigm of object-oriented programming. Personally I find such diversity fascinating!

3.4   Recap of Ideas

As we draw near the conclusion, let's quickly go over what we've covered:

- The object-oriented paradigm is one way to envision a runtime system, allowing you to understand and control it.

- According to this paradigm, a runtime system is full of happy objects, jumping about, and doing work, all in order to solve your problem!

- Classes typically play a passive role during runtime, being useful mostly during the system's design and construction.

- Recognizing the distinction between the significance of objects and that of classes is important because it can impact design and implementation choices.

- You can model your system using an object-focused approach instead of a class-focused one, deriving benefits of a lax and open system where objects can interact promiscuously.

- Breaking away from inheritance, especially complex relationships, is a good step; remember that the roles played by an object are more interesting than the classifications that exist in the domain.

- Test-driven development guides you toward an object-focused design.

- Certain languages provide features that give objects a first-class status. Ruby exposes classes as objects that are manipulatable at runtime. JavaScript completely does away with the class concept, dealing only with objects.

- Exploring language support like mixins, metaprogramming, prototypes, and so on, can help clean up your code base and improve team productivity. These techniques aren't just for framework writers!

3.5 Wrapping Up

The final question that arises is, "Where should we stand with respect to objects vs. classes?"

There isn't a definitive answer. You'll have to take your own call. But I'll conclude with how I've come to look at these concepts.

What is an object? It's something that takes birth, exhibits some behavior, interacts with other objects, and finally dies off or is simply forgotten, all in an effort to solve a problem.

What is a class? It's a container for related behavior that a new object can start off with.

What is not a class? It's not the fundamental building block of an object-oriented system: that's what objects are for! A class should be neither an enforcement of a contract nor a limitation on how objects can behave.

Why should we use classes?

- Classes improve the structuring and readability of code and hence the maintainability of a system.

- Classes are a way of grouping related behaviors and giving them a name from the domain and can thus become a tool for communication within teammates and with business stakeholders.

- Classes help envision and comprehend a frozen snapshot of what would otherwise be moving parts of a very dynamic system.

These reasons are *soft* benefits. The hard benefits may be achieved without classes in some programming languages. Either way, the soft benefits can act as guiding principles. A simple indicator of the proper use of classes is when you don't feel locked down by the class-related choices you've made and the objects in your system are free to move about and interact with whoever they need to, without restriction.

You know what? You and I are free to move about too, to continue exploring the exciting world of programming, looking out for the next language that challenges us and invokes in us a desire to step back and *think!*

CHAPTER 4

Functional Programming Techniques in Object-Oriented Languages

by Marc Needham

Functional programming languages have grown in popularity over the past few years, which has popularized some useful programming techniques that we can use even if our language of choice is predominantly object-oriented.

While the ideas behind functional programming have become popular only in the past couple of years, the underlying platform features that allow us to program in a functional way in C# have been built into the CLR since around 2005.

The C# language has evolved since then to the point where we can write code in C# that looks quite similar to that which could be written in F#—Microsoft's functional programming language that has recently been made a first-class language for Visual Studio.

The functional programming ideas[1] themselves have been around for at least half a century.

In this essay, we'll demonstrate these techniques with examples in C# and Ruby, although the ideas presented are also applicable in other similar languages such as Scala and Java.

---

1.   http://en.wikipedia.org/wiki/Functional_programming

4.1   Collections

When it comes to understanding how a functional approach to problem solving can be used, one of the first things to consider is the way that we view collections.

The Transformational Mind-Set

The most interesting mental paradigm switch when learning how to program in a functional way is how you deal with collections.

With an imperative approach, you think about each item in the collection individually, and you typically use a for each loop when working with that collection.

If we take a functional approach to solving problems with collections, our approach becomes much more about viewing the collection as a whole—something that Patrick Logan refers to as a *transformational mind-set*.[2]

We look at the original collection that we have and then visualize how we want it to look once we've transformed it, before working out which functions we need to apply to the collection to get it into that state.

Original -> () -> () -> () -> Final

It closely resembles the pipes and filters architecture where the data moves through a pipe, and the filters are represented by the different functions that can be applied to that data.

Our approach to dealing with collections in this way is possible by using what Bill Six calls *functional collection patterns*.[3]

There are three main categories of operations on collections.

Map

The *map* pattern applies a function to each element in the collection and returns a new collection with the results of each function application (see Figure 1, *The Map Function*, on page 73). Therefore, if we want to get the first names of a group of people, we would write the following code:

```
var names = people.Select(person => person.FirstName)
```

rather than the following imperative equivalent:

---

2.   http://www.markhneedham.com/blog/2010/01/20/functional-collectional-parameters-some-thoughts/#comment-30627
3.   http://www.ugrad.cs.jhu.edu/~wsix/collections.pdf

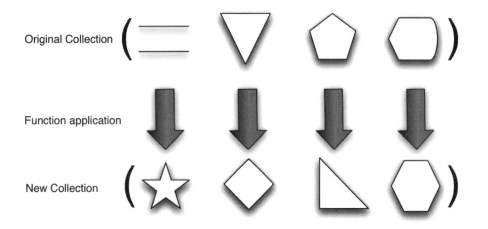

Figure 1—The Map Function

```
var names = new List<string>();
foreach(var person : people)
{
    names.Add(person.FirstName);
}
```

Filter

The *filter* pattern applies a predicate to each element in the collection and returns a new collection containing the elements that returned true for the predicate provided.

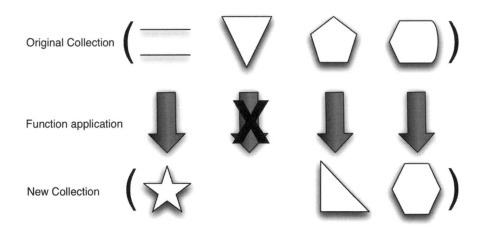

If we want to get only the people older than twenty-one years old, we would write the following code:

```
var peopleOlderThan21 = people.Where(person => person.Age > 21);
```

which is again simpler to read than the following imperative equivalent:

```
var peopleOlderThan21 = new List<Person>();
foreach(var person : people)
{
    if(person.Age > 21)
    {
        peopleOlderThan21.Add(person);
    }
}
```

Reduce

The *reduce* pattern converts a collection to a single value by combining each element in turn via a user-supplied function.

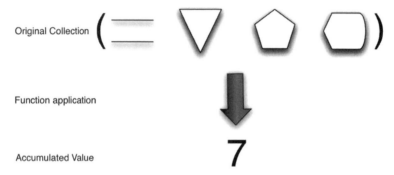

If we want to get the ages of a group of people, we would write the following code:

```
var sumOfAges = people.Aggregate(0, (sum, person) => sum + person.Age);
```

as compared to this:

```
var sumOfAges = 0
foreach(var person : people)
{
    sumOfAges += person.Age;
}
```

Embracing Collections

Once we get into the habit of applying functions to collections, we start to see more opportunities to use a collection where before we might have used a different approach.

Quite frequently I've noticed that we end up with code that more closely describes the problem we're trying to solve.

To take a simple example, if we wanted to get a person's full name, we might write the following code:

```
public class Person
{
    public string FullName()
    {
        return firstName + " " + middleName + " " + lastName;
    }

}
```

which works fine, but we could write it like this instead:

```
public class Person
{
    public string FullName()
    {
        return String.Join(" ", new[] { firstName, middleName, lastName });
    }
}
```

In this case, it doesn't make a lot of difference, and there's not that much repetition in the original version. However, as we end up doing the same operation to more and more values, it starts to make more sense to use a collection to solve the problem.

A fairly common problem I've come across is comparing two values against each other and then returning the smaller value. The typical way to do that would be as follows:

```
public class PriceCalculator
{
    public double GetLowestPrice(double originalPrice, double salePrice)
    {
        var discountedPrice = ApplyDiscountTo(originalPrice);
        return salePrice > discountedPrice ? discountedPrice : salePrice;
    }
}
```

But instead we could write it like this:

```
public class PriceCalculator
{
    public double GetLowestPrice(double originalPrice, double salePrice)
    {
        var discountedPrice = ApplyDiscountTo(originalPrice);
        return new [] { discountedPrice, salePrice }.Min();
    }
}
```

The second version is arguably easier to understand because the code reads as return the minimum of discountedPrice and salePrice, which perfectly describes what we want to do.

Don't Forget to Encapsulate

One unfortunate side effect of the introduction of the LINQ library and the consequent ease with which we can now work with collections is that we tend to end up with collections being passed around more than we would have previously.

While this isn't a problem in itself, what we've seen happen is that we'll get a lot of repetition of operations on these collections that could have been encapsulated behind a method on the object that the collection is defined on. The other problem with passing around collections is that we can do anything we want with that collection elsewhere in the code.

We worked on a project where it became increasingly difficult to understand how certain items had ended up in a collection because you could add and remove any items from the collection from multiple places in the code.

Most of the time, it's unlikely that the domain concept we're trying to model with a collection actually has all the operations available on the C# collection APIs. LINQ typically gets the blame when these problems occur, but it's more a case of it being used in the wrong place.

The following is a typical example of passing around a collection:

```
company.Employees.Select(employee => employee.Salary).Sum()
```

We could easily end up with the calculation of the employees' salaries being done in more than one place, and our problem would be increased if we added more logic into the calculation.

It's relatively easy to push this code onto the Company class.

```
public class Company
{
    private List<Employee> employees;
    public int TotalSalary
    {
        get
        {
            return employees.Select(employee => employee.Salary).Sum();
        }
    }
}
```

Sometimes it makes sense to go further than this and create a wrapper around a collection.

For example, we might end up with a Division that also needs to provide the TotalSalary of its employees.

```
public class Division
{
    private List<Employee> employees;
    public int TotalSalary
    {
        get
        {
            return employees.Select(employee => employee.Salary).Sum();
        }
    }
}
```

We can create an Employees class and push the logic onto that.

```
public class Employees
{
    private List<Employee> employees;
    public int TotalSalary
    {
        get
        {
            return employees.Select(employee => employee.Salary).Sum();
        }
    }
}
```

We've frequently seen a lot of resistance to the idea of creating classes like this, but if we start to have more logic on collections, then it can be quite a good move.

Lazy Evaluation

JavaScript sees extensive usage of its language. One problem that we can very easily run into when using iterators is evaluating the same bit of code multiple times.

For example, we might have the following code reading a list of names from a file:

```
public class FileReader
{
    public IEnumerable<string> ReadNamesFromFile(string fileName)
    {
        using(var fileStream = new FileStream(fileName, FileMode.Open))
```

```
            {
                using(var reader = new StreamReader(fileStream))
                {
                    var nextLine = reader.ReadLine();
                    while(nextLine != null)
                    {
                        yield return nextLine;
                        nextLine = reader.ReadLine();
                    }
                }
            }
        }
    }
}
```

which is then referenced from our PersonRepository.

```
public class PersonRepository
{
    private FileReader fileReader;
    IEnumerable<Person> GetPeople()
    {
        return fileReader.ReadNamesFromFile("names.txt")
                        .Select(name => new Person(name));
    }
}
```

It's used elsewhere in our code like so:

```
var people = personRepository.GetPeople();
foreach(var person in people)
{
    Console.WriteLine(person.Name);
}

Console.WriteLine("Total number of people: " + person.Count());
```

The file actually ends up being read twice—once when printing out each of the names and then once when printing out the total number of people because the ReadNamesFromFile() method is lazy evaluated.

We can get around that by forcing eager evaluation.

```
public class PersonRepository
{
    private FileReader fileReader;
    IEnumerable<Person> GetPeople()
    {
        return fileReader.ReadNamesFromFile("names.txt")
                        .Select(name => new Person(name))
                        .ToList();
    }
}
```

4.2 First-Class and Higher-Order Functions

A higher-order function is one that takes in another function or returns a function as a result. We've seen plenty of examples of the former in the previous section.

Functions (lambda expressions) are first-class citizens in C#; we can use them in any place where we can use any other language entity. In fact, they are converted into delegates by the compiler and are merely syntactic sugar available to the developer at design time.

One thing the lambda syntax does give us is the ability to pass around functions much more easily.

The only thing we need to be careful with when passing around functions is ensuring that we'll still be able to understand the code when we come back to it later. It's very easy to write code that is completely incomprehensible when we start to make heavy use of the Func() and Action() delegates. One way to save ourselves some of the pain is to create named delegates to describe what the function actually does.

For example, if we were passing around the following function:

```
public class PremiumCalculator
{
    public Money CalculatePremium(Func<Customer, DateTime, Money> calculation)
    {
        // calculate the premium
    }
}
```

then we could replace each use of that function with the following delegate:

```
public delegate Money PremiumCalculation(Customer record, DateTime effectiveDate);
```

and then change the CalculatePremium() method to take in the delegate, like so:

```
public class PremiumCalculator
{
    public Money CalculatePremium(PremiumCalculation calculation)
    {
        // calculate the premium
    }
}
```

It's not a match for match replacement, so we can't move the code across to this solution incrementally—we'll now have to go and change all the places that we were passing in a function to pass in the delegate instead.

Simplifying Gang of Four Patterns

One of the nice side effects of being able to pass around functions is that we're able to massively reduce the amount of code that we need to write in order to implement some of the patterns from *Design Patterns: Elements of Reusable Object-Oriented Software [GHJV95]*.

On a recent project, we wanted to find a generic way of caching the results of any request to around twenty to thirty web services that we were able to do with the following code, a variation of the *Decorator* pattern:[4]

```
public class ServiceCache<TService>
{
    protected readonly TService service;
    private readonly ServiceCache cache;
    public ServiceCache(TService service, ServiceCache cache)
    {
        this.service = service;
        this.cache = cache;
    }
    protected TResp FromCacheOrService<TReq, TResp>(Func<TResp> service, TReq req)
    {
        var cached = cache.RetrieveIfExists(typeof(TService), typeof(TResp), req);
        if (cached == null)
        {
            cached = service();
            cache.Add(typeof(TService), req, cached);
        }
        return (TResp) cached;
    }
}
```

Since we're able to pass a function to the FromCacheOrService() method, we do not need to add an abstract method to ServiceCache that each cached service would need to implement.

We can then use ServiceCache like so:

```
public class CachedPaymentService : ServiceCache<IPaymentService>, IPaymentService
{
    public CachedPaymentService(IPaymentService service, ServiceCache cache)
            : base(service, cache) {}

        public PaymentResponse GetPayment(PaymentRequest params)
        {
            return FromCacheOrService(() => service.GetPayment(params), params);
        }
}
```

---

4.   http://en.wikipedia.org/wiki/Decorator_pattern

4.3 Minimizing State

One of the other key ideas behind functional programming is that of avoiding mutable state in our applications.

This is done by creating *values* rather than *variables*. In functional programming languages, you typically wouldn't be able to change a value once it has been created; in other words, values are immutable.

It's difficult and somewhat nonidiomatic to write code that is completely immutable in object-oriented languages, but we can still make our programs easier to understand by mutating state less frequently.

For example, hashes in Ruby are typically built like this:

```
delivery_costs = {}
[:standard, :next_day, :same_day].each do |type|
  cost = DeliveryService.calculate_delivery_cost(delivery_address, type)
  delivery_costs[type] = "%.2f" % cost
end
```

In this version of the code, we're creating a variable called delivery_costs and then mutating it inside the each loop.

In this case, there's probably not much problem with that, but if the definition of delivery_costs ends up moving away from the place where it's actually populated, then we can end up quite confused about the state of the variable.

We could encapsulate that mutation with the following code, which uses the reduce() method:

```
delivery_costs = [:standard, :next_day, :same_day].reduce({}) do |result, type|
  cost = DeliveryService.calculate_delivery_cost(delivery_address, type)
  result[type] = "%.2f" % cost
  result
end
```

We could still go on and mutate delivery_costs elsewhere in the code if we wanted, but at least the initial creation and population process doesn't involve mutation of that variable.

Another way that we can help reduce state in our applications is by performing calculations only when we actually need the result[5] rather than doing so ahead of time and storing the result in a field.

I've come across the following style of code fairly frequently:

---

5. http://www.markhneedham.com/blog/2009/09/02/coding-reduce-fields-delay-calculations/

```
public class PaymentService
{
    private double monthlyPayment;
    private double yearlyPayment;

    public PaymentService(ExternalService externalService)
    {
        this.monthlyPayment = externalService.CalculateMonthlyPayment();
        this.yearlyPayment = externalService.CalculateYearlyPayment();
    }

    public double MonthlyPayment()
    {
        return monthlyPayment;
    }

    public double YearlyPayment()
    {
        return yearlyPayment;
    }
}
```

We don't actually need to know the monthlyPayment or the yearlyPayment unless the user of PaymentService makes a call to the appropriate methods.

We've also unnecessarily created state in the PaymentService class.

Instead of doing that, we can store the externalService and then calculate the payment values when needed.

```
public class PaymentService
{
    private ExternalService externalService;

    public PaymentService(ExternalService externalService)
    {
        this.externalService  = externalService;
    }

    public double MonthlyPayment()
    {
        return externalService.CalculateMonthlyPayment();
    }

    public double YearlyPayment()
    {
        return externalService.CalculateYearlyPayment();
    }
}
```

One argument against transforming the code like this is that we might end up making more calls to ExternalService, but if we do get to the stage where that's a problem, we can deal with it then.

4.4 Other Ideas

The following are a few other ideas.

Continuation Passing Style

Now we can start to use things like Continuation Passing Style (CPS), where we pass the rest of the computation as a function.

A simple example of CPS would be the following identity function:

```
static void Identity<T>(T value, Action<T> k)
{
    k(value);
}
```

which we might use like so:

```
Identity("foo", s => Console.WriteLine(s));
```

Here we've passed the remaining computation—in this case, just a print statement—to the Identity() function, which passes control of the program to that function.

In a more interesting example,[6] I converted the following controller code to follow CPS:

```
public ShoppingController : Controller
{
  public ActionResult Submit(string id, FormCollection form)
  {
    var shoppingBasket = CreateShoppingBasketFrom(id, form);

    if (!validator.IsValid(shoppingBasket, ModelState))
    {
      return RedirectToAction("index",
          "ShoppingBasket", new { shoppingBasket.Id });
    }
      try
      {
        shoppingBasket.User = userService.CreateAccountOrLogIn(shoppingBasket);
      }
      catch (NoAccountException)
      {
        ModelState.AddModelError("Password", "User name/email invalid");
```

---

6. http://www.markhneedham.com/blog/2010/03/19/functional-c-continuation-passing-style/

```
        return RedirectToAction("index", ""Shopping", new { Id = new Guid(id) });
    }

    UpdateShoppingBasket(shoppingBasket);
    return RedirectToAction("index", "Purchase", new { Id = shoppingBasket.Id });
    }
}
```

using an idea I've seen in jQuery code where you pass success and failure functions as callbacks to other functions.

```
public class ShoppingController : Controller
{
  public ActionResult Submit(string id, FormCollection form)
  {
    var basket = CreateShoppingBasketFrom(id, form);
    return IsValid(basket, ModelState,
      failureFn: () => RedirectToAction("index", "Shopping", new {basket.Id}),
      successFn: () =>
        Login(basket,
          failureFn: () => {
            ModelState.AddModelError("Password", "User name/email invalid");
            return RedirectToAction("index", "Shopping", new {Id = new Guid(id)});
          },
          successFn: user => {
            basket.User = user;
            UpdateShoppingBasket(basket);
            return RedirectToAction("index", "Purchase", new {Id = basket.Id});
                  }));
  }

  private RedirectToRouteResult IsValid(ShoppingBasket basket,
                                        ModelStateDictionary modelState,
                                        Func<RedirectToRouteResult> failureFn,
                                        Func<RedirectToRouteResult> successFn)
  {
    return validator.IsValid(basket, modelState) ? successFn() : failureFn();
  }

  private RedirectToRouteResult Login(ShoppingBasket basket,
                                      Func<RedirectToRouteResult> failureFn,
                                      Func<User,RedirectToRouteResult> successFn)
  {
    User user = null;
    try
    {
      user = userService.CreateAccountOrLogIn(basket);
    }

    catch (NoAccountException)
    {
```

```
    return failureFn();
  }

  return successFn(user);
  }
}
```

The common theme in this code seemed to be that there were both success
and failure paths for the code to follow depending on the result of a function,
so I passed in both success and failure continuations.

I quite like that the try/catch block is no longer in the main() method, and the
different things that are happening in this code now seem grouped together
more than they were before.

In general, though, the way I read the code doesn't seem that different.

Instead of following the flow of logic in the code from top to bottom, we just
need to follow it from left to right, and since that's not as natural, the code
is more complicated than it was before.

4.5   Wrapping Up

One of the hazards of using an object-oriented language every day is that it
seeps into your thinking. Embracing different paradigms allows you to see
problems differently. I illustrated that many on-the-fly concatenations are
really just list transformations; thinking about them in that way allows us to
treat them more as first-class citizens. Think of collections as transformations,
and you might find that you are solving a broader problem than you thought
or, better yet, someone has already solved it for you.

You can also use these techniques to simplify design patterns. I showed how
using different building blocks such as higher-order functions allows you to
think about problems and their solutions differently. Learning any new programming paradigm is useful because it broadens your palette of approaches.
Functional programming offers a lot of innovative ways to solve old problems.

Part II

Testing

Five ThoughtWorkers explore the intersection of agile and technical topics with essays on extreme performance testing, JavaScript testing, and acceptance testing.

XP takes commonsense principles and practices to extreme levels.

➤ *Kent Beck*

CHAPTER **5**

Extreme Performance Testing

by Alistair Jones and Patrick Kua

Agile methods play a key role in our project work with clients every day. Our clients' software systems often demand high levels of performance, but we have found very little Agile literature aimed at the subject, and what we did find failed to directly answer the question, "How do agile methods apply to performance testing?"

Our combined experience on more than twenty Agile projects helped us apply Agile values and principles[1] to performance testing. We have evolved a set of concrete working practices that have proved successful for our clients. We hope that you can benefit from these practices, so we describe them here, under the term *Extreme Performance Testing*. The term is inspired by *Extreme Programming (XP) [Bec00]*; XP has a strong influence in our work and places unique emphasis on the engineering practices needed to make Agile work.

5.1   Stating the Problem

Software development teams have always been concerned with performance. Over the years, focus has shifted from making features possible on the modest hardware available to making features scale as load increases. However, the concerns remain similar—we have to implement a long list of features, while at the same time worrying in the back of our minds about whether the software will perform as desired. The recent advent of cloud computing is also starting to make the cost of computing resources more explicit, and we are starting to see a corresponding focus on software performance.

---

1.   As described on http://www.agilemanifesto.org

Conventionally Disjoint Performance Testing

Where a software project includes performance testing, we often see it being planned as a distinct project phase, scheduled after development and before deployment to production. In *The Art of Application Performance Testing [Mol09]*, Ian Molyneaux describes a rigorous process that follows this pattern. He characterizes performance testing as a project in its own right, consisting of the following:

- Requirement capture
- Test environment build
- Transaction scripting
- Performance test build
- Performance test execution
- Analyze results, report, retest

Performance testing projects of this kind are suitable for outsourcing to an external supplier. Alternatively, many organizations have a dedicated performance testing team that provides performance testing as a service to projects as required. The common theme is that performance testing is a separate activity from the task of writing software, and there is a separate team responsible for it.

The motivations for this separation are as follows:

- Performance testing is seen as a certification process, so it is logically grouped with other activities (such as user acceptance testing) that happen in the run-up to deployment.

- Performance testing requires specialist skills, and it is considered more efficient to concentrate those skills in a single-purpose team rather than to raise skills to the required level in a general-purpose team.

Extreme Programming and Agile Software Development

Over the past decade, Agile methods have become popular for software development teams. These methods feature iterative and incremental development, close customer involvement, and regular prioritization and planning. Agile teams aim to keep their software in a constantly releasable state,[2] so testing effort is included in the cost of delivering features. Agile teams have an integrated testing capability so that they can verify functionality as it is developed and measure productivity in terms of tested features delivered.

---

2.   See the inspiration for daily deployment in *Extreme Programming Explained [BA04]*.

This contrasts with a traditional model, where testing is conducted by a separate team.

In addition to these management practices, XP recommends a number of supporting engineering practices. These practices increase discipline and quality in the development process so that working software is assured and iterative development is practical.

However, performance testing is not one of the activities specifically mentioned by XP, and there is no clear guidance from the Agile community for how to integrate it with the development process. In our early Agile projects, we found it being run as an independent activity outside of the core development team. Performance testing remained outside of the iterative development process and operated as a waterfall stage after development and before release.

Weaknesses of Disjoint Performance Testing

A common weakness of disjoint performance testing is that it comes too late. While many projects express a desire to start performance testing early, in reality it is very hard to schedule performance testing until after most development is complete. If performance testing is scheduled too early in the project, then the software will not be complete enough for the results to be meaningful. On the other hand, if it starts too late, then any negative results will require significant rework, with the potential to delay release. It may be possible to break up performance testing effort into small chunks and schedule these chunks throughout the project life cycle. However, if a specialist team must be mobilized for each of these chunks, there is a significant overhead in getting it up to speed each time, and scheduling commitments for multiple teams will be challenging.

Another aspect to consider is that performance testing requires a deep understanding of the system under test.

- Performance tests must be designed to accurately reflect how the system will be used.

- Tests must be executed against the right technical components of the system.

- When tests do not work as expected, troubleshooting is required.

- Diagnosis of performance bottlenecks requires knowledge of the system architecture and software design.

If the performance testing team is independent from the development team, it will have to spend time gaining the required level of knowledge or seek assistance from the development team that has the required knowledge. This effort is in addition to the performance testing itself and can take a great deal of time for a complex system. When the development team is itself under stress trying to deliver more features, the performance testing team will have trouble getting access to the required knowledge, which will put the success of the performance testing effort at risk.

For management, it is difficult to decide how much time and resources to assign to performance testing. The performance testing team will need to be set up, or their time reserved in advance, before it is known whether there will be any significant performance issues. If the initial performance results are positive, it should be possible to redirect future performance testing capacity toward developing additional features, but by this time, it is too late to change direction; the performance team is not experienced at developing the software. Conversely, if many performance issues are encountered, the time scheduled for performance testing will be exceeded, and multiple projects could be delayed. The best management can do is take an educated guess.

In summary, separate performance testing is difficult to schedule at the right time in a project, it has a large communication overhead, and it has a high risk of either wasting resources or delaying projects.

5.2   A Different Approach

In recent software development projects with demanding performance requirements, we experimented with an alternative to the traditional model of separate performance testing. With our experience of Agile and Extreme Programming, we could see how the principles of Agile methodologies could be applied to the adjacent realm of performance testing. We put forward the principle that performance testing should be integrated into the main development effort, and we derived a set of supporting practices. Following these practices has been very successful, so we are now able to recommend the approach to other projects.

Single Multidisciplinary Team

We recommend that a single team should be responsible for both software development and performance testing. This team will have a similar makeup to a typical XP team and contain team members specializing in analysis, in development, and in testing.

Compared to a development team without performance responsibilities, some additional skills in performance testing are required, but we do not suggest having team members who exclusively do performance testing. Instead, a number of team members should have performance testing skills in addition to their other skills. We find that developers or testers commonly hold or can easily acquire these skills.

What does it mean to create such a team? First, it means removing physical division between performance testing and development; both activities should happen in the same room. However, one room does not imply one team. When performance testing work is needed, it should not always be the same people who do it. Going further, there should not even be a subset of the team that can take on performance work; all developers and all testers in the team should actively contribute to performance testing on a regular basis.

A typical Agile development team might be organized, as shown in Figure 2, *Separate performance testing team*, on page 94, alongside an independent performance testing team. We recommend pulling down the wall between these teams and forming a single development team, as shown in Figure 3, *Integrated development and performance testing team*, on page 94.

We recommend team members with performance testing skills *pair program* with others so that their specialist skills will spread to other team members. Growing a larger pool of people equipped with specialist performance testing skills reduces the risk that performance testing stops because one person is unavailable. It also gives the team greater flexibility to put much more effort into performance testing later in the project, should such a change of focus be required.

A team without division will have lower communication overhead, will accelerate the spread of knowledge, and will foster a culture of shared purpose.

Expressing Requirements

We find that *user stories* are an effective way of capturing performance requirements. Agile teams will be familiar with using a standard structure for writing stories, such as the "so that, as a, I want" pattern. Consistent patterns like this have the clear advantage of calling out the motivation and owner of every story. For performance testing stories, we find it useful to add clauses such as "when" or "while" to emphasize the conditions under which a certain target needs to be met.

Two distinct kinds of stories are relevant to performance. First, there are stories that express requirements on the system itself, such as supporting a specific load in a specific scenario. They are what most people think of when they think of performance requirements. Here is an example of such a story:

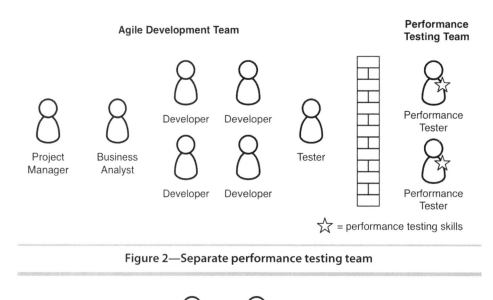

Figure 2—Separate performance testing team

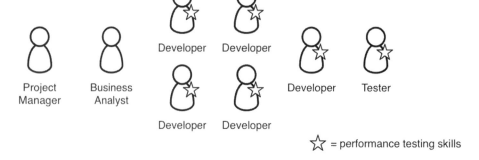

Figure 3—Integrated development and performance testing team

So that investors have a high-quality experience as the business grows,

as the Operations Manager,

when 10,000 users are logged in and viewing 1 portfolio value page, which refreshes every 2 seconds,

I want the portfolio value page to render within 0.2s.

When the team comes to play this story, they will need to measure the performance of the system as it stands and then re-measure as they make any required performance improvements. The measurement requires a high-quality test that may take significant effort to create. We find it useful to separate the work of creating the test from the work of improving system performance.

This leads us to the second kind of performance story: the test-implementation story. Test-implementation stories express what stakeholders want to measure about the system. Here's an example:

> *So that* I can determine whether further development work is required,
>
> *as the* Operations Manager,
>
> *I want* a reusable performance test that measures response time for investor operations,
>
> *while* simulating the load of at least 10,000 logged-in users.

There is a clear dependency between the test-implementation story and the system-performance story: the test-implementation story should be played first. For a complex system, it may be necessary to play a number of test-implementation stories, building a set of measurement tools required to measure and improve performance.

It makes sense to keep test-implementation and system-performance separate because

- Test-implementation stories can be played on their own. It is independently valuable to be able to measure performance, even if system-performance targets are not yet known.

- It is easier to measure progress and identify what is taking development time. The clear division makes it convenient to track time spent building a test vs. time spent improving performance.

Performance stories have the same structure and share many characteristics with conventional feature stories. Therefore, they can follow the same workflow as the project's other stories: they should be generated, analyzed, implemented, and verified using the same process. They will live in the same backlog, ready for planning and prioritization.

Small-Enough Units of Work

One characteristic of a good story is being small.[3] In our experience, performance testing stories typically consume more time than a typical functional story in the same project, so you want to do all that you can to split them into small stories. Smaller stories allow for faster feedback and make it easier to adjust plans as you get more information about how long they are taking to implement.

---

3. This is the *S* in INVEST criteria, as described in *User Stories Applied [Coh04]*.

Some of the techniques for splitting performance stories are not so different from the methods used for splitting functional stories.[4]

You may have a number of different performance scenarios under which you need to measure performance, especially scenarios that involve different load profiles. Rather than set up all scenarios in one story, why not implement the simplest scenario first (for example, a steady background load) and then add the more sophisticated scenarios (for example, a series of sudden spikes triggered by market activity) as later stories that incrementally enhance the original test?

A spike is time-boxed investigation that sets out to answer a specific technical question. Spikes can be useful in performance testing where significant uncertainly remains. For example, "Will our current performance testing tool be able to generate enough load to simulate this scenario?" is an appropriate question to answer through a spike. After completing the spike, subsequent stories have a lower risk and will be easier to estimate and plan.

Where sophisticated visualization is required to interpret test results, implement a simple visualization first, and then enhance. For example, plot one variable first, and then enhance the visualization with more diagnostic data.

Planning and Prioritization

Performance stories will be worked on by the same people who could otherwise develop features, so all the stories should be placed in the same backlog or story list. Performance work can be prioritized against feature development, which is a powerful tool to give to your stakeholders. Maybe for the first release performance is not very important, because the user numbers are expected to be small. In this situation, your stakeholders may choose to defer the majority of performance work to a later release. Stories provide a mechanism for making this kind of trade-off explicit. The *Performance Champion*, on page 99 works to help prioritize performance stories with the XP customer.

Thanks to the automated orchestration and Continuous Performance Testing practices described next, tests implemented early can continue to be run throughout the project without incurring extra effort, so performance work is not wasted even if the software is far from being complete when the tests are implemented. A given iteration is likely to include a mixture of performance and feature stories. An example of how performance stories could be played

---

4. See the techniques described by Rachel Davies at http://agilecoach.typepad.com/agile-coaching/2010/09/ideas-for-slicing-user-stories.html.

alongside feature stories over the course of a project is shown in Figure 4, *Performance stories played in each iteration*, on page 97.

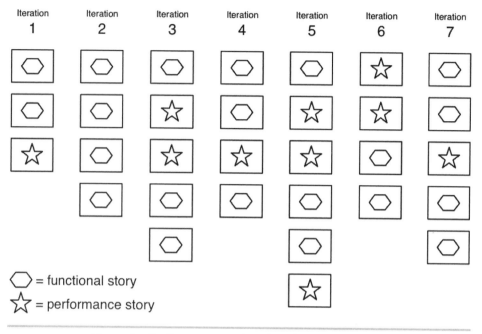

Figure 4—Performance stories played in each iteration

The normal criteria for ordering stories apply to performance stories: the stories that deliver the most value should be played early, while at the same time the riskiest stories should be played early to reduce uncertainty. When applied to performance, this means we should prioritize tests for the scenarios that deliver the most business value and also prioritize tests that validate the riskiest technical decisions. When ordering performance stories against feature stories, you should consider that you risk significant rework until the basic architecture has been validated from a performance perspective, so a basic level of performance stories should have been played before the bulk of feature stories.

Playing Performance Stories

A snapshot of a typical story wall is shown in Figure 5, *Typical story life cycle*, on page 98. The life cycle for a performance story should be similar to that of a feature story; they should both move through all the states on the story wall.

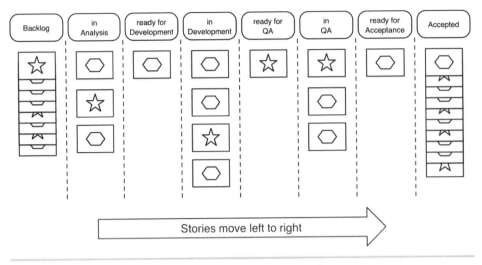

Figure 5—Typical story life cycle

In feature development, each story will have acceptance criteria, which are written down at an appropriate time before development starts. These acceptance criteria serve as a definition of "done," and there is a phase after development is complete (a QA phase) where the acceptance criteria are validated independently from the developers. This formality should still apply to performance stories; acceptance criteria should still be agreed on before work starts, and they should be independently verified after work is complete (by someone who did not do the bulk of the work).

When a test-implementation story is being played, the acceptance criteria will require checking that the test does put the system under the load advertised and that the results displayed match independently verifiable numbers. When a system-performance story is being played, the acceptance criteria will be about conducting the tests under the right controlled conditions and correctly interpreting the results.

Showcases and Feedback

Performance stories should be included in the team's regular showcases. This gives visibility of the work that has gone into performance testing and gives stakeholders better information for their prioritization of future performance work. Graphs and charts of performance test results are particularly suitable for presenting at a showcase.

5.3 Extreme Performance Testing Practices

Extreme Performance Testing presents a new set of challenges compared to separate performance testing, and different practices are required to support the approach. At the same time, Extreme Performance Testing offers opportunities for practices that improve the efficiency and effectiveness of performance tests themselves. This section describes practices that we have found to work well when a team is practicing Extreme Performance Testing.

Performance Champion

XP uses the XP *Customer* role to prioritize work based on business value. People who take on this role are often from the business and consequently do not have a technical background to think about the cost of performance. Sites like Google, Twitter, and Facebook do not scale for free. Without being more informed about performance costs, the XP Customer will continue to prioritize building new features over making investments to meet performance requirements.

The *Performance Champion* role complements the XP Customer role. It does not replace it. The Performance Champion's responsibilities include:

- *Educating others on performance*: Businesspeople often do not understand the many types of performance traits such as latency, responsiveness, and throughput, among others. The Performance Champion works with other roles to help educate what each performance trait is and often what various trade-offs might be. They help other roles understand what additional effort might be needed to reach certain orders of magnitude in one performance trait.

- *Contributing to the prioritization process*: Neglecting performance testing and tuning puts risk on the business. The Performance Champion works to help highlight the risks created by neglecting performance traits critical to their software systems. The ideal outcome is a balanced prioritization between incremental and iterative delivery of new features and performance testing.

- *Knowing when enough is enough*: Defining a target for each performance trait is important to establish how much effort to invest in performance testing. An application for ten users is significantly different from an application designed for Internet-scale use, and someone must create a model for each performance trait.

- *Defining a contingency strategy*: Businesses sometimes make a choice to avoid investing in performance tuning because the risk is low. However, when they make such a choice, someone needs to define how the application gracefully degrades.

Automated Deployment

All software projects benefit from automated deployment; it removes manual error, ensures consistency, and enables more frequent releases. When following Extreme Performance Testing, automated deployment becomes even more valuable. In software projects that follow separate performance testing, we see that a significant time that has been allocated to performance testing is actually spent deploying the application to a performance testing environment. The deployment process itself is often time-consuming, and since the performance testing environment is seldom used, a lot of time can also be spent ensuring that the environment is configured correctly and that the application functions as expected.

In Extreme Performance Testing, automated deployment occurs before each performance test run. It eliminates the cost of upgrading the application and allows rapid feedback on the impact of changes in the code. It should be easy to deploy a new version, run a test, and compare results.

The technology used for deployment will usually be scripts that transfer software artifacts to appropriate servers and then trigger installation. Realistic hardware is required for performance testing, and this is likely to mean more application servers than in development environments; the automation should cover upgrading all the application servers at the same time. The most realistic hardware is generally located outside the office network, possibly in a production data center. When this is the case, more sophisticated scripts will be needed that are capable of operating through the strict security barriers that are appropriate between an office network and a production data center. Where on-demand computing resources are available (when using a public or private cloud), automated deployment should also include automated acquisition of suitable computing resources on which to run the application.

In addition to installing the application itself, deployment scripts should also install the load-generating agents required to run performance tests. It is not sufficient to manually install load-generating agents and leave them in place; over time, their configuration will drift apart, and the agents will become a maintenance nightmare. Cut this off early by automating installation so that a clean, consistent set of agents is ready for the start of each test.

Automated Analysis

Performance testing tools produce results in the form of log files or reports. After each test run, these results must be analyzed to answer questions such as "Is the performance acceptable?" We recommend automating this analysis of test results so that there is no manual work required to answer key questions about the test. Where available, the analysis capabilities of the performance testing tool can be automated. Otherwise, it is worthwhile to write a small amount of software to analyze results according to the specific requirements of the application under test.

Extreme Performance Testing runs many more tests than what is possible for disjoint performance testing. Many more log files result, and without automation, the cost of analyzing results becomes significant.

Automation also creates more consistency in analysis. Once written, scripts interpret test results the same way all the time. People are more prone to making mistakes, adding risk by missing problems, or spending time chasing nonexistent anomalies. Elimination of manual errors is best achieved through automation.

Result Repository

Performance test results are valuable. A *result repository* stores and organizes performance test results so that you can get the most value from them over the life of the application.

For each performance test run, the full *raw results* should be captured, alongside reference data, such as the following:

- The time and duration of the test run.

- The scenarios executed as part of the test run.

- The exact version of the software the test ran against (this should be traceable to a specific revision in source control; a date or version number is insufficient).

- Details of the environment in which the application was deployed and details of the agents used to generate load. Where the hardware or config- uration of the environment changes over time, it's important to keep track of these changes alongside test results.

The result repository should capture both raw result data and the output from automated analysis. It's valuable to keep the raw data because if you enhance analysis capabilities over the course of the project, you can go back and reanalyze raw data from historical tests. Meanwhile, it's useful to store output from analysis, because analysis may itself be time-consuming, and it would be inconvenient to repeat it simply to find out the result of a historical test.

A well-structured result repository will support historical analysis. It allows you to ask questions such as, "Has our application always exhibited this behavior?"

There are a number of different technical options for how to implement a result repository. On past projects, we have made use of the artifact repository of our Continuous Integration server to store test results, because this makes it extremely easy to keep track of the exact version of software against which the test was run. Alongside the artifact repository, we track historical trends in a simple relational database, including references back to the underlying raw data. We do not recommend storing test results in a source control system; these tools are not designed for storing this kind of data, and they can become quickly overwhelmed by the sheer volume of raw data.

In conventional performance-testing approaches, results are frequently distributed via email, and looking for historical trends means searching through your inbox. It is generally only the specialist performance testing team that has access to the raw data. By implementing a formal result repository, you can open up access to the data and get better value out of the test results.

Result Visualization

Regularly running performance tests produces a huge amount of data. Trawling through data line by line or the results from a twelve-hour run is extremely difficult, error-prone, and subjective. Communicating trends or a performance characteristic is even more difficult when dealing with these large sets of data, with someone often acting as an interpreter.

Visualizations are important for understanding the results of a test performance run. Unusual characteristics on a visual draw the eye more than a large number among a mass of other numbers. We tend to favor graphs because most performance tests have some sort of time-based nature.

Avoid generating a single graph per test run. Graphing too much data makes the chart more difficult to interpret. Keep a graph focused on a smaller set of elements and generate more graphs to visualize different elements separately. Chapter 12, *A Thousand Words*, on page 197 provides many more guidelines on how to visualize data more effectively.

Automated Test Orchestration

Test orchestration is the set of steps that need to be followed to successfully start, run, and stop a performance test run. Here is an example recipe for running a performance test:

1. Deploy application.

2. Wait for deployment to be complete (frequently deployment is an asynchronous operation, and it is necessary to wait until it is actually ready to service requests).

3. Start load generator(s) (if a high load is required, then multiple load generators on isolated hardware may be required, and this step must coordinate all the load generator instances).

4. Wait for a bedding-in period (frequently, an application gives unrepresentative results soon after starting, and it is common practice to hit the application with a small number of requests over a bedding-in period, before starting the main performance test).

5. Increase load (load level determined by the test plan).

6. Wait for a measurement period (again, the time that each load level is sustained is determined by the test plan).

7. Repeat steps 5 and 6 until the test plan is complete (the test plan may include a number of steps of increasing or reducing load).

8. Stop the load generator(s).

9. Optionally, stop the application, and free up any temporarily allocated hardware.

10. Collect performance test results.

A comprehensive performance testing tool will include automation of changing load to match a performance testing plan. However, a performance testing tool has the bias of seeing the process from the point of view of the load generators. When considering test orchestration, we find it important to consider the whole testing process, including the important role of the application. Orchestration should include anything that has to happen to the application, such as waiting for it to start up, waiting for it to bed in, and so on. There should be no special tricks known only to performance testers about how to get a good result. Any special knowledge should be captured and become an automatic part of the orchestration.

Once all test orchestration is automated, the goal is that tests should run unattended. In the general case, there is no need to sit watching a performance test running. The team should feel confident that, once triggered, a performance test will run to completion without intervention and that everything will be cleaned up at the end.

Sanity Test

The nature of performance testing involves long cycles of feedback. A single test may run for as short as an hour or as long as week. A single error invalidating a test run wastes time better spent analyzing or running other tests. The *sanity test* extends the Agile idea of *failing fast*. The sanity test does this by running a full cycle of the performance testing process at a reduced rate or capacity. The aim of these tests is to test the performance testing process. A successful sanity test detects errors in the performance testing process as early as possible. Sanity tests are small investments that maximize the value received from an expensive testing environment by guaranteeing that test runs are useful and valid.

Without any validation, errors creep into automated processes easily. One common problem during performance testing is errors in deployment or an application incorrectly configured. A simple sanity test in this context is an automated test that runs against the environment for an extremely short period of time just to validate a successful deployment and that the application exhibits the expected behavior for the test. This sort of test is particularly useful for systems developed without any automated test coverage. Performance is meaningless if the application does not work.

Having many individual components and disparate application processes makes the performance testing process brittle. Copying or archiving the results of a performance test run is often a problem area, with small errors such as log files spit out to a different directory on a different machine or automation failing to generate the final reports. A performance test run is wasted if there is no output. In this situation, a short, automated sanity test validates that the performance testing process generates the appropriate artifacts. For example, at one client, the post-build process of a test run included generating an archive file of results. This file contained images representing visualized test results alongside the original raw test data and details about the environment the test ran in. Waiting for a long performance test to complete to find out that the automation of this process was broken was wasteful. The sanity test saved us many times; it uncovered subtle bugs in the bespoke scripts that generated all the files necessary for this archived process to run successfully much faster.

Detecting memory leaks is much harder to pick up with a sanity test; however, it is still possible with VM-based programs by determining a maximum memory usage for a small data set and then starting the application with a constrained maximum heap size.

Continuous Performance Test

Continuous Performance Testing extends *Continuous Integration [DMG07]*. Conventional Continuous Integration validates that an application builds and meets its functional requirements. Regressions detected trigger immediate feedback to the development team. Continuous Performance Testing adds another criterion to Continuous Integration by ensuring that the application meets its performance requirements. Any new performance issues are flagged as soon as possible.

Continuous Performance Testing builds on top of the practices of automated deployment, automated analysis, and automated test orchestration. Continuous Performance Testing adds an additional stage to the application's build pipelines that deploys the latest version of the application, executes performance tests, and verifies that the application meets its performance targets. If performance targets have not been met, then the build stage will fail, and the development team will be alerted by the normal methods of Continuous Integration. It is also possible to automatically set performance targets based on the results of previous tests, failing the build stage if performance has regressed by a certain fraction in comparison to previous results.

Continuous Performance Testing's main benefit is the ability to identify code changes that cause performance regressions very soon after the code change has been made. This allows the developers who made the change to investigate and fix the problem while the change is still fresh in their memory, and if the design is flawed, the team can avoid building further functionality that will suffer from the same problem.

Disciplined Performance Enhancement

When performance tests show that the application meets its performance requirements, no additional effort is required to improve performance. When these same tests demonstrate an application failing its performance requirements, the tests take on a secondary role to help diagnose and fix performance problems.

In this performance diagnosis and improvement role, we recommend a high level of discipline, following a process inspired by the *Scientific Method [Gau02]*. Without this discipline, it's common for a development team to lose track of what has changed between test runs, to be unsure of the impact of the changes they have made, and ultimately to make unnecessary or unhelpful changes to the software.

We recommend that disciplined performance diagnosis and improvement be structured as a series of well-defined cycles. A suitable performance enhancement process is shown in Figure 6, *Performance enhancement cycles*, on page 106.

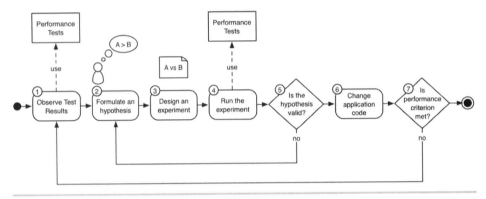

Figure 6—Performance enhancement cycles

The important thing to notice about this process is the clear distinction between forming a hypothesis and making long-term changes to the application. Without this distinction, you cannot be sure that code changes will actually improve performance, and you risk making changes that introduce unnecessary complexity or even changes that degrade performance.

In the past, we have seen teams making a number of performance-related changes at the same time and testing their impact using a single performance test run. This is unsatisfactory because it's not possible to determine the impact of the individual changes.

Following *disciplined performance enhancement* may seem like a lot of work, but it is made much easier by the other practices of Extreme Performance Testing. In particular, automation of most of the steps in the cycle makes it much faster to repeat them several times, and therefore it becomes practical to isolate each individual change and measure its impact in a realistic test.

5.4 How This Helps You

So, how does this help you?

Better Performance

The earlier you find performance problems, the easier they are to fix. Practices like *Continuous Performance Test*, on page 105 immediately detect the small change that breaks performance targets. Detecting problems earlier removes the cost involved in tracking down what particular set of changes caused a problem, and efforts can be better spent on working out a better solution.

Less Complexity

When you have better integration between a performance testing team and the other aspects of development, it reduces duplication in effort. Reusing existing automated test fixtures for performance testing fixtures means less code to write and maintain. Any application interface changes affect only a single set of code.

Just as *Test-Driven Development [Bec02]* improves the design of code, *Performance Test–Driven Development* improves the system design. The heavy emphasis of automation in Extreme Performance Testing forces developers to consider scriptable hooks into applications, configuration, and the deployment process, often making other tasks such as monitoring much simpler.

Greater Team Productivity

We find it beneficial to have continuity between development and performance testing. Rather than the traditional model of handing off a finished application to a separate performance testing team, the integrated approach uses the same team for both activities, so detailed knowledge of the application can be used to help performance testing. In the separate performance testing approach, care must be taken to schedule the performance testing team to be available at a specific point in the larger process, which introduces risk and is quite inflexible should project timelines need to be modified.

Improved Prioritization

Extreme Performance Testing gives stakeholders a much richer set of choices about how much to invest in performance testing, more options for when to make the investment, and better information with which to make investment decisions. Instead of choosing whether to engage a performance testing team (and if so, for how long), stakeholders can choose fine-grained units of performance testing and prioritize them against feature development. Also, decisions about how many performance testing stories are played can be made based on existing performance test results. If fewer performance targets are met early in the project and no improvement cycles are required, then additional capacity will be available for feature development.

Enabling Continuous Delivery

In *Continuous Delivery [HF10]*, Jez Humble and David Farley describe how to smoothly deliver working software to production on a regular basis. Extreme Performance Testing can be seen as a supporting practice for continuous delivery. Automated performance tests play a similar role to automated regressions suites: they lower the cost of certifying that software is suitable for release, thereby enabling more frequent releases.

5.5   Wrapping Up

We have tested the techniques described in the chapter on real projects with good results. Extreme Performance Testing is ready for more people to use.

Extreme Performance Testing will not be suitable for every team in every situation. If you are considering adopting Extreme Performance Testing, we recommend that your development team should already be practicing an Agile methodology and should have strong engineering skills, as advocated by XP. It also makes sense to start with a project that has significant performance challenges so that you can get the most out of the practices and give a good amount of experience to all team members.

We are looking forward to more teams adopting Extreme Performance Testing. We expect that others will improve the practices and adapt them to their own needs. Most importantly, we want to see teams building lots of high-performing applications!

CHAPTER 6

Take Your JavaScript for a Test-Drive

by Brian Blignaut and Luca Grulla

In the past few years the Web has moved away from being a platform for simply displaying static content toward a platform for delivering rich Internet applications. Extensive DOM manipulation and Ajax callbacks are now fundamental to every Web 2.0 application. JavaScript is the de facto language that has allowed this to happen.

Unfortunately, though, the JavaScript side of the code base rarely receives the same level of attention with regard to testing that the back-end systems do, and this can result in client-side code that is hard to maintain and enhance, resulting in an inconsistent and error-prone experience for the user.

In this essay, we will discuss our approach to writing and testing client-side JavaScript in the context of large web projects.

6.1 The JavaScript Renaissance

Since its inception, JavaScript has always been treated as a second-class language by most developers, and as a result, the coding practices haven't evolved at the same rate as they have in other more established languages, even though the size and complexity of JavaScript code bases have grown enormously over the last few years.

In addition, with the explosion of Web 2.0, several JavaScript libraries have emerged and defined a new approach to client-side JavaScript development. Libraries such as jQuery[1] have helped developers abstract away some of the difficulties of web development (such as cross-browser issues) and have increased developers' productivity with features such as DSL-style selectors and advanced animations. This additional power has also increased the

---

1.   http://jquery.com

complexity of the code: a mix of fluent interface APIs and the use of advanced selectors are promoting a coding style that can be more concise but also very hard to read and evolve.

Lastly, the additional capabilities of modern JavaScript engines and advanced features of HTML5 are enabling user experience designers and developers to unleash the potential of the Web with richer user interfaces and interactions. Advanced features such as local storage—which allows applications to be used offline—are going to push web applications further down the route of being rich client applications, with browsers becoming hosting environments.

It's therefore clear that there is a need for solid engineering practices and approaches to keep this new complexity under control, to sustain an organic growth of the code base, and to avoid a spaghetti code style of JavaScript. We also need practices that will help us avoid regression and help us evolve the code release after release.

Unit testing is a well-established practice that helps us achieve internal software quality and reduce defect rates. Unit tests work at a very low granularity, focusing on a specific component in isolation from its collaborators. The key element is isolation: if we can focus on a specific behavior while ignoring all the additional complexity of the rest of the system, the test will be very specific, and in the case of an error, it will be very easy to identify the broken area and fix it.

6.2 Current JavaScript Approach and Problems

The nature of client-side JavaScript is event-driven: the user interacts with a component on the screen (such as clicking a button), and the application executes some actions and shows some new or additional information to the user.

In too many JavaScript code bases, the event handler—that acts as the entry point in the system—is often overloaded with responsibilities. In the same callback function, we can find data manipulation, DOM transformations, and server communication via Ajax calls all merged together.

The code also tends to operate at a very low level, with a lack of modeling around the domain and the more fundamental functional layers. The Java-Script ends up being so coupled to the DOM that the only way to test the JavaScript layer is by using HTML fixtures. Because DOM manipulations are often used to display the result of some Ajax calls, the JavaScript code ends up being coupled not only with the DOM but also with the server, which must be serving data from the whole application stack.

This scenario leads to two problems.

First, the code can be tested only as a black box, and for web applications this means acceptance tests at the browser level. Browser-based acceptance tests have a lot of value when used to test specific application scenarios but tend to be slow and brittle when used to test isolated areas of functionality in an application and therefore are not the ideal way to test JavaScript. They are also too high level for what we are trying to do: if an acceptance test fails, it could be because of a problem in any of the application layers, because acceptance tests tend to exercise the application as a whole.

Second, we incur code crystallization. When the code is entangled without a clear design, it's very difficult to evolve and add new functionality, leading to duplications and often to more unneeded complexity.

6.3 Separation of Concerns

Let's take a look at some code (from now on we'll use jQuery—with its standard $ notation—as a core JavaScript library).

```
JavaScriptTesting/loginPage.js
function LoginPage() {
    this.setup = function() {
        $("#loginButton").click(this.login)
    },

    this.login = function (e) {
        var username = $("#username").val();
        var password = $("#password").val();

        if (username && username !== "" && password && password !== "") {
            $.ajax({
                url: "/login",
                type:"POST",
                data:{username:username, password:password},
                success: loginPage.showLoginSuccessful,
                error: loginPage.showLoginError
            });
        } else {
            loginPage.showInvalidCredentialsError();
        }
        e.preventDefault();
    },

    this.showLoginSuccessful = function() {
        $("#message").text("Welcome back!");
        $("#message").removeClass("error");
        $("#message").fadeIn();
    },
```

```
    this.showInvalidCredentialsError = function() {
        $("#message").text("Please enter your login details");
        $("#message").addClass("error");
        $("#message").fadeIn();
    },

    this.showLoginError = function() {
        $("#message").text("We were unable " +
                            "to log you in with the details supplied");
        $("#message").addClass("error");
        $("#message").fadeIn();
    }

};

$(document).ready(function() {
    var loginPage = new LoginPage();
    loginPage.setup();
});
```

This is a very simplified version of a login script. It performs input validation and then attempts to log the user in using the supplied credentials. The code that comprises the previous business logic would be as follows:

- The user input validation
- The steps that are followed depending on the outcome of the validation
- The login attempt

The rest of the code has to do with our presentation logic and integration logic.

As things stand, the previous code is pretty readable, ignoring the violation of the Single Responsibility Principle (SRP).[2] But what if our validation logic suddenly becomes more complicated? Or for that matter, what if the business owner decides they want the messages to be displayed to the user in a manner that requires a number of animations and effects? As the code stands now, accommodating these features would result in a mess of spaghetti code that was almost impossible to test without setting up an entire HTML fixture and exercising the code from end to end. While this is certainly an option, we would have no guarantees that the fixture would be representative of the true state of the HTML used in production, meaning we could potentially end up with a false positive with regard to the state of our application.

So, how should we go about solving the problem?

---

2.   http://butunclebob.com/ArticleS.UncleBob.PrinciplesOfOod

Just as with any other language, separation of concerns plays a big role in writing readable, testable, and maintainable JavaScript.

If we are therefore able to identify and isolate the different roles and responsibilities in our code, we will be able to create components that collaborate to achieve the specific functionality that we are implementing, instead of an entangled set of low-level instructions. Components will promote encapsulation and enforce SRP, making the code flexible and easy to change and formalizing *contracts* between the objects via the API that we are creating.

What we are striving to achieve is to isolate the areas of our code that comprise distinct areas of functionality. By separating these distinct areas, we allow ourselves the ability to use standard unit testing approaches such as mocking and stubbing[3] to test the application without requiring complex HTML fixtures. This approach also helps us ensure that our code remains loosely coupled, which in turn brings with it all the usual benefits with regard to refactoring.

Looking carefully at the previous example, we can see how our JavaScript code is executing the core business logic (username and password validation) and then *sending messages* (executing function calls) to the server (via HTTP) to validate the user credentials and then to the DOM to update the information shown to the user.

And what are DOM and HTTP with respects to the business logic if not integration points?

The business logic is calling the server over HTTP in the same way our server-side code would talk to another system via a web service. Our client-side JavaScript is definitively integrating with the server, and the code used for the integration (that is, to make the Ajax calls happen) is our anticorruption layer.[4]

Again, from a business logic point of view, the DOM is an integration point. The business logic is actually using the DOM loosely as a datastore: it fetches information from a node, it updates nodes and change their attributes, and it adds and remove nodes. We could say that the JavaScript layer is interacting with the DOM via CRUD operations.

If we see the DOM and the HTTP as integration points, we are actually defining two very clear boundaries of the system, and consequently we start identifying the separation of the business logic from the rest of the system. From a testing

---

3. For a detailed explanation of the differences between stubs and mocks, check out Martin Fowler's article at http://martinfowler.com/articles/mocksArentStubs.html.
4. http://c2.com/cgi/wiki?AnticorruptionLayer

point of view, with these boundaries in place, we can mock the external dependencies from our core business logic, actually removing the dependencies of the business logic code from the browser (in the form of the DOM) and the server. We now have three very clear abstractions.

Presentation

> The presentation abstraction is all about how we display the application to the user. For example, things like making sure that each alternate row in a table is highlighted correctly or that validations have the correct icon next to the message are presentation issues. You should typically try to ensure that areas of common functionality related to presentation are grouped together to ensure that they applied consistently across the application, thus ensuring the user is provided with a consistent view.

HTTP

> The HTTP abstraction is responsible for the integration with the server. The obvious candidate here would be any Ajax calls required; however, this would include web sockets[5] if the application was making use of them.

Application Logic

> This is the code that is at the core of our application. The rules with regard to how the application functions are treated as application logic. This includes things like the validation rules being applied and also what we do based on user input.

Most standard web applications will easily fall into this model.

The abstractions defined previously are fairly close to the well-known Passive View pattern.[6] We would like to highlight how the Passive View pattern is a suitable solution for this problem, but every application may have different needs and therefore may need different abstractions. The important thing is to ensure that you split your application into distinct areas of responsibility.

With these concepts in mind, we can now refactor our code, pulling out the right abstractions.

JavaScriptTesting/loginPageLogic.js

```
function LoginPageLogic(view, authenticationService) {
    this.init = function() {
        view.addLoginHandler(this.validateCredentials)
    };
```

---

5. http://en.wikipedia.org/wiki/WebSockets
6. http://martinfowler.com/eaaDev/PassiveScreen.html

```
    function credentialsAreValid(username, password) {
        return (username && username !== "") && (password && password !== "");
    }


    this.validateCredentials = function() {
        var username = view.getUsername();
        var password = view.getPassword();


        if (credentialsAreValid(username, password)) {
            authenticationService.login(username, password,
                    view.showLoginSuccessful, view.showLoginError);
        }else {
            view.showInvalidCredentialsError();
        }
    }
}
```

with the *wiring* code that now looks like this:

```
JavaScriptTesting/loginPageLogic.js
$(document).ready(function() {
    var serviceUrl = "http://localhost/authentication";
    var authService = new AuthenticationService(serviceUrl);
    var loginPageView = new LoginPageView();
    var loginPageLogic = new LoginPageLogic(loginPageView, authService);
    loginPageLogic.init();
});
```

LoginPageLogic now clearly represents the business logic that we want to execute; all the interactions with the server and with the UI have been pushed respectively to AuthenticationService and to LoginPageView.

With the core logic so nicely isolated, we can now think about writing tests around this section of the code. In particular, we can write interaction tests, using a mocking library to validate that the expected interactions between LoginPageLogic and its collaborators are actually happening.

Using JSTestDriver[7] as a unit testing tool and JSMockito[8] as a mocking library, we can now start writing a test that will validate that the right callback is invoked when AuthenticationService returns with no errors.

```
JavaScriptTesting/tests/loginPageLogicTests.js
test_calls_auth_service_with_correct_callbacks : function() {
    var loginPageViewMock = mock(LoginPageView);
    var authServiceMock = mock(AuthenticationService);
```

---

7. http://code.google.com/p/js-test-driver/
8. http://jsmockito.org/

```
    var loginPageLogic = new LoginPageLogic(loginPageViewMock,
                                            authServiceMock);
    loginPageLogic.init();

    when(loginPageViewMock).getUsername().thenReturn("username");
    when(loginPageViewMock).getPassword().thenReturn("password");

    loginPageLogic.validateCredentials();

    verify(authServiceMock).login(is(equalTo("username")),
                        is(equalTo("password")),
                        is(equalTo(loginPageViewMock.showLoginSuccessful)),
                        is(equalTo(loginPageViewMock.showLoginError))
                        );
}
```

We can also write a test that validates that the right error message is shown to the user if the credential validation fails.

```
JavaScriptTesting/tests/loginPageLogicTests.js
test_shows_login_error_if_password_not_entered:function() {
    var loginPageViewMock = mock(LoginPageView);

    var loginPageLogic = new LoginPageLogic(loginPageViewMock, null);
    loginPageLogic.init();

    when(loginPageViewMock).getUsername().thenReturn("username");
    when(loginPageViewMock).getPassword().thenReturn("");

    loginPageLogic.validateCredentials();

    verify(loginPageViewMock).showInvalidCredentialsError();

}
```

These two tests are specifically exercising the business logic, with no dependencies on server-side code or the DOM. This is the core of the system and what we really want to validate. We do this by verifying that all the collaborators are called correctly and validating that the messages' orchestration works as expected.

What do the identified collaborators look like?

We identified and introduced two collaborators.

- LoginPageView
- AuthenticationService

The code for AuthenticationService is as follows:

JavaScriptTesting/authenticationService.js

```
function AuthenticationService(serviceUrl) {
    this.login = function(username, password, successCallback, errorCallback) {
        browser.HTTP.post(serviceUrl, {username:username, password:password},
                          successCallback, errorCallback);
    };
}
```

with:

JavaScriptTesting/browser.js

```
browser.HTTP = {
    post : function(url, myData, successCallback, errorCallback) {
        $.ajax({
        url: url,
        type:"POST",
        data:myData,
        success: successCallback,
        error: errorCallback

        });
    }
}
```

This is pretty straightforward. To authenticate the credentials, we need to communicate with the server via an Ajax call. browser.HTTP() is just a simple wrapper to reduce the low-level call verbosity.

LoginPageView is more interesting.

JavaScriptTesting/loginPageView.js

```
function LoginPageView() {
    this.getUsername = function() {
        return $("#username").val();
    };

    this.getPassword = function() {
        return $("#password").val();
    };

    this.addLoginHandler= function(callback) {
        $("#loginButton").click(function(e) {
            e.preventDefault();
            callback();
        });
    };

    this.showLoginSuccessful = function() {
        browser.Animations.showMessage("#message", "Welcome back!");
    };
```

```
    this.showInvalidCredentialsError = function() {
        browser.Animations.showError("#message", "Please enter your login details");
    };

    this.showLoginError = function() {
        browser.Animations.showError("#message",
                "We were unable to log you in with the details supplied");
    };
}
```

LoginPageView is the gateway for every operation on the UI.

Its real value is not in its responsibilities (it shouldn't actually have any responsibilities)—it's all in the semantic value that it adds to the rest of the code (business logic and tests).

Looking at the tests, we can now see that they are easy to follow and understand because LoginPageView is talking the views' domain language, expressing *what* we want to do and not just *how* we want to do things.

Without this layer, business logic and tests will talk directly to jQuery, reducing the expressiveness of the code and resulting in tests that are hard to follow and maintain.

The view should then be as skinny as possible, with simple delegation to other lower-level collaborators. With such a trivial implementation, there is no real need for testing this object, and any emergent need for testing logic in the view should be treated as a code smell (this would be indicative of logic that should be moved to the business layer).

But not all the operations we want to execute on the UI are of the same complexity. Sometimes it's a one-line operation, but more often it would be a set of operations on the DOM that make sense only when executed as a whole.

For basic operations, we are happy to talk directly to the lowest level of our JavaScript stack (that is, jQuery); however, when working with a set of operations that need to be performed repeatedly as a whole, we prefer to isolate these interactions into functions grouped into a separate namespace, that is, browser.Animations.

JavaScriptTesting/browser.js
```
browser.Animations = {
    showMessage : function(selector, message) {
        $(selector).text(message);
        $(selector).removeClass("error");
        $(selector).fadeIn(2000);
    },
```

```
    showError : function(selector, error) {
        $(selector).text(error);
        $(selector).addClass("error");
        $(selector).fadeIn(2000);
    }
}
```

These functions are fundamental to the user experience. Imagine having duplication of showMessage() all over the place: if, for example, we need to change the duration of the fading animation from 2,000 milliseconds to 3,000, we may miss some of them, and this will result in an inconsistent journey for the end user, which will ultimately reduce the perceived quality of the application. By extracting these functions, we not only follow the DRY principle,[9] but we are also able to test this functionality at a very low level. In this case, we do want to write a test that validates the low-level interaction with the DOM (and so the *integration* with it), and we will use an HTML fixture to set up and validate the behavior.

JavaScriptTesting/tests/browserDisplayTests.js
```
TestCase("BrowserDisplayTests", {
    test_show_error_displays_error_correctly: function() {
        /*:DOC += <div id="message" class="message"></div> */
        browser.Animations.showError("#message", "error message");
        assertEquals($("#message").text(), "error message");
        assertTrue($("#message").hasClass("error"));
    }
});
```

In this test, once the fixture is defined[10] and the function under test is invoked, we assert against specific node attributes to validate that the manipulations applied to the DOM are successful.

6.4 Our Testing Approach

We can now summarize the approach we like to take when dealing with client-side JavaScript.

Favor Interaction Tests over Integration Tests

The approach we just described is clearly promoting an interaction testing style rather than an integration-based approach.

In client-side JavaScript, we consider integration tests to be those tests that require specific setup like having a DOM available or a server up and running

---

9. http://c2.com/cgi/wiki?DontRepeatYourself
10. We are declaring the fixture using JSTestDriver comment syntax.

to be executed. If a test needs an HTML fixture before it can be run, it is an integration test (in this case with the DOM). In the same way, if a test needs a server to reply to Ajax calls, it is an integration test (it's testing the integration with HTTP and the specific server).

With such a clear isolation of concerns, we can then focus our testing on verifying that our application logic is sending the right messages to the other collaborators and components in a pure interaction-based testing style. We believe that client-side JavaScript libraries shield us enough from different DOM implementations in different browsers and that there is not enough return on investment from having full test coverage on this part of the system. The critical part of our JavaScript that requires the most testing is the business logic and the orchestration between the presentation layer, the server layer, and our business logic.

Write Integration Tests with HTML Fixtures in Very Specific Cases

We also recognize that HTML fixtures are just another representation of code duplication and that they tend to go out of sync with the original front-end markup very quickly. It's true that we could try to write a very generic fixture to make that HTML snippet more resistant to change, but this will reduce the domain specificity of the test, making it less valuable as a form of documentation. We believe that a well-written test is in fact often more expressive than any other form of written documentation, and we appreciate how the context defined via the test setup is critical for the expressiveness of the test. An out-of-sync (or too generic) HTML fixture results in a test where it is hard to determine what the intention of actual test is.

Of course, there are scenarios where integration tests and the use of HTML fixtures are important.

As shown in the example, we like to validate complex UI interactions (several DOM operations to achieve a single effect) using fixtures. We also like to use fixtures when we have to rely on advanced selectors to traverse the DOM to fetch specific nodes. In our experience, this is a typical cross-browser issue, and Internet Explorer 6 and 7 (and sometimes also more modern browsers) have let us down on more than one occasion. Having a test that we can run on all our target browsers helps ensure that the functionality performs as expected and helps avoid regression.

Use Acceptance Tests to Validate That Everything Hangs Together

With JavaScript, we prefer to work at the unit test level, and this won't easily cover the binding of events to the right HTML components.

In our experience, an error in this area is very rare; the chances to attach the wrong event to a component are very low and usually picked up very quickly during development. We therefore don't feel the need for extensive testing in this area. In our overall testing strategy, we generally have a few browser-based acceptance tests that will verify the main scenarios. Working at the UI level, these are automatically validating (even if at very high level) that the most of the handlers are correct.

Joe asks:
Can I TDD My JavaScript?

Of course, you can TDD your JavaScript code.

As soon as you stop thinking about JavaScript as just another hackable language, all the design and coding techniques that you are already familiar with will become available.

6.5 Continuous Integration

Now that we have tests, we certainly want to run them as part of our build to have the best possible feedback at each check-in. JavaScript tests are very fast to run, and hundreds can be executed in a matter of seconds.

6.6 Tools

At the time of writing, there is still a lot of active evolution in the JavaScript tools landscape, with no one tool necessarily standing out as the standard (yet). The key decision point for us is that each chosen tool should be easy to integrate with our Continuous Integration server.

For testing, we prefer tools that use real JavaScript engines and ideally run tests in multiple browsers. As described, we prefer interaction tests over integration tests, but we believe that it's critical for our testing strategy to run the few integration tests we have with an HTML fixture in the target browsers.

Unit Testing

JSTestDriver[11] is a tool with a very simple and neat syntax, excellent integration with Continuous Integration servers, a simple yet powerful configuration, and the ability to execute the tests in a variety of browsers in parallel.

---

11. http://code.google.com/p/js-test-driver/

Syntax Checking

An important tool to use is a syntax checker; our favorite tool right now is JavaScriptLint.[12] It is simple to use and highly configurable with regard to what you want checked.

The bare minimum thing to check for is that there are no missing semicolons in the code (because minification[13] and compression may not work correctly otherwise), but most of the tools available are highly configurable in terms of what has to be checked. Because the syntax check is so important (and fast), we like to execute it as the very first step in our build pipeline. If our code doesn't pass this initial check, there is no need to even start with other more expensive tasks like compilation (yes, we run this before compiling the server-side code) or functional and acceptance tests.

Mocking Framework

With such a strong focus on interaction testing, a good mocking library is essential. We need a tool where we can define expectations on function calls as well as defining the return values for these function calls. One of our favorites is JSMockito. It takes inspiration from Mockito,[14] a well-known Java mocking library, with a simple syntax and powerful integration with JSHamcrest[15] matchers that make our assertions extremely readable.

6.7 Wrapping Up

The advent of HTML5 and the focus on rich Internet applications is going to result in a vast shift in the type of applications available on the Internet. It is only by ensuring that the code we write is capable of evolving that we will be able to guarantee that we can provide the best possible user journey while meeting our business requirements. With the increasing focus on JavaScript as a first-class language and the growth in rich Internet applications, we as developers need to start focusing on writing JavaScript that is not only concise but also readable, testable, and maintainable. Through the application of good design practices, we therefore ensure that the applications we write today are future proof.

---

12. http://www.javascriptlint.com
13. http://en.wikipedia.org/wiki/Minification_(programming)
14. http://mockito.org/
15. http://jshamcrest.destaquenet.com/

CHAPTER 7

Building Better Acceptance Tests

by James Bull

Certain issues arise frequently when writing automated acceptance test suites; they can be slow, brittle, and unmaintainable. By the end of this essay, you should have a good idea of how to create tests that are fast, resilient, and maintainable. We'll also look at how acceptance testing fits in with the wider software development process and how this can influence the adoption of the good practices mentioned here. The examples will all be from website testing, but the advice should be broadly applicable.

We begin with a definition. An acceptance test is all of the following:

- Driven through the user interface
- Run on the full software stack
- Run on an environment with real integration points where possible
- Fully automated
- Run as part of your Continuous Integration build

Our goal in acceptance testing is to increase confidence in the suitability of the product for release at any time and to significantly reduce the time spent performing manual regression testing.

7.1 Fast Tests

Fast tests are good because they allow us to get feedback on the quality of the code more often. The more builds you can run your tests against, the better. The longer it takes to get feedback on a particular change, the longer you can have a bug in your system without realizing it. It's difficult to quantify exactly what "too slow" is, but if you can't run your tests or a useful subset of them several times a day, then they would benefit significantly from being sped up.

Base Your Tests Around User Journeys

Because acceptance tests are slower to run than unit tests, you will probably find it difficult to test everything with acceptance tests and have them run quickly enough. Automated acceptance tests should form part of our overall automated test strategy. All of the assertions we are going to make in these tests should be tested at the unit level; when we test through the user interface, we are not trying to test all the edge cases but trying to see whether all the layers of the application work together to create a coherent whole.

Target tests at the most frequently used functionality. Pick the most vital parts of the system and try to test the main paths through those parts. One effective way of doing this is to consider the journey a user will take through the system to achieve the system's primary goal.

Begin by developing a number of personas who represent a cross section of your typical users, and imagine how they might use the site. To work out where to start, consider what the business goal of the site is, and focus on that.

For example, if we consider the ThoughtWorks website, the personas we identify might include the following:

- *Curious developer Dave*: Interested in ThoughtWorks processes
- *Potential client Clive*: Interested in previous client experiences

Create a journey through the system for each persona that typifies the user we are considering. The test should follow exactly what the user in these examples would do. In this case, we could have Dave visit the careers section of the website while Clive views a selection of client experience reports.

This differs from a more traditional approach because it covers more of the system in a single test. Of course, this brings with it the same drawbacks that you would normally hope to avoid by breaking up your tests into small parts. You may find that it is less obvious what has broken in your code because there are more things that could fail, thus causing your test to break. This is mitigated, though, by the fact that everything covered here also has unit tests covering the same code in more detail at a lower level.

The advantage this approach brings in terms of speed is that unlike tests that focus on a small part of the system and visit the same pages, many times we hit each page only once and take a single journey through the system, thus keeping execution time to a minimum.

Parallelize Test Suite Execution

To do this, we could use a tool such as Selenium Grid. This, however, results in tying us to a specific tool because it works only with Selenium tests. This approach works best when we have an existing Selenium test suite we are looking to speed up.

A better idea if we are using a different tool is to make it easy to run a subset of tests. That way, we can check out our code onto multiple boxes and run different sections of the suite on different machines and parallelize that way. It should be possible to take advantage of most Continuous Integration software to do this and get a comprehensive test report at little cost. Where this is not possible, we may have to go to a little more trouble and manually deploy different configuration files to different machines and have them all write their reports to a common network share. You can easily split up test suite execution without writing too much code. Here I have used a naming convention to make it easy to run different tests. If you look at the examples, I have called the tests DeveloperDaveUserJourneys and ClientCliveUserJourneys. This allows me to run the tests for any particular user or all journeys by using the Ant jUnit task.

```
BuildingBetterAcceptanceTests/AnthologyAcceptanceTests/build.xml
<target name="test" depends="compile">
    <junit printsummary="yes" haltonfailure="no"
           showoutput="true" fork="yes" forkmode="perBatch">
        <jvmarg value="-Dweb.driver=${driver.type}"/>
        <classpath refid="classpath"/>
        <formatter type="plain" usefile="false" />
        <batchtest>
            <fileset dir="${test.dir}">
                <include name="**/*${tests.to.run}*.java" />
            </fileset>
        </batchtest>
    </junit>
</target>
```

Consider Using Multiple Test-Drivers

One thing to consider is multiple implementations of our browser driver interface. By this I mean that rather than write your tests to use your tool directly, you should declare an interface and write your tests to that and then provide an adapter that will actually hand off the calls to the tool. This allows you to have more than one driver implementation for your test suite.

Have one implementation that drives a browser and one that does not. Run the tests through the browser for greater confidence, and run them with a non-GUI-based driver for increased speed. This allows more tests to be run before check-in while still running the full suite through a browser as part of our CI build.

One tool that uses this approach already is WebDriver. It has a number of implementations, including support for HTMLUnit, Chrome, Internet Explorer, and Firefox. The example tests use WebDriver, and I have used a static class called ApplicationTestEnvironment to get all the pages I will be testing and inject the appropriate driver. The driver type is passed into the tests on the command line and passed into the JVM as a property, as you can see in the previous example.

There are two methods.

BuildingBetterAcceptanceTests/AnthologyAcceptanceTests/src/Utilities/ApplicationTestEnvironment.java

```java
public static Object getPage(Class c){
    try {
        Page p = (Page) c.newInstance();
        p.setDriver(getDriver());
        return p;
    } catch (InstantiationException e) {
        e.printStackTrace();
    } catch (IllegalAccessException e) {
        e.printStackTrace();
    }
    return null;
}
```

This method is called by the tests when they want to get hold of a page they will interact with. It calls getDriver() to get hold of an appropriate implementation of WebDriver.

BuildingBetterAcceptanceTests/AnthologyAcceptanceTests/src/Utilities/ApplicationTestEnvironment.java

```java
private static WebDriver getDriver(){
    String driverType = System.getProperty("web.driver");
    if(driverType.equals("browser")){
        if(driver==null){
            driver=new FirefoxDriver();
        }
        return driver;
    }
    else{
        HtmlUnitDriver newDriver =  new HtmlUnitDriver();
        //newDriver.setJavascriptEnabled(true);
        return newDriver;
    }
}
```

This allows you to select both the tests and the driver used to run them easily from the command line. A simple batch file such as this one...

BuildingBetterAcceptanceTests/AnthologyAcceptanceTests/Test.bat
```
ant -Ddriver.type=%1 -Dtests.to.run=%2 test
```

allows you to run tests from the command line. The following three examples run one user through the browser, the next example illustrates using the headless HTMLUnit driver, and the next journeys through the browser.

```
Test browser Dave
Test headless Clive
Test browser UserJourneys
```

This sort of setup allows us to easily choose which driver to use and run the same tests in a different way.

There are some potential pitfalls with this approach. If your site is JavaScript-heavy and will not work without JavaScript enabled, then you are less likely to have luck with HTMLUnit because it uses a different JavaScript engine from a browser. By default WebDriver does not enable JavaScript in the HTMLUnit driver, so if you require it, you may be better off just using the full browser driver. If you decide to do this, then you get access to various functionality that is available only on full browser drivers such as hover.

I have been on a project where we successfully made use of a headless driver on a site that makes significant use of JavaScript. We did have a specific requirement to work with JavaScript disabled, though, and progressively enhance the website where JavaScript was available. This combined with a decision from the beginning that this was going to be the automated test strategy to use made it work for us.

Have Separate Test Runs

If you have structured your test suite effectively, run it in parallel, and taken advantage of a headless driver and you still want to speed up your tests, then consider maintaining two test runs.

Run one set of high-risk tests as part of your main build, and use this subset as your active test set for normal development activity. The rest of the tests can then run either in parallel on a separate "slow build" pipeline or, if you have limited build environments, overnight. If a test in the slow test breaks, then move it into the active set. If a test has been in the active set without breaking for some time, then you can consider moving it into the low-risk test set.

You could do this through a naming convention like we used earlier, but if you find you need finer control over which tests are run, then you could go to a little additional effort and have all your tests individually referenced in a configuration file and then write some code that examines the last x build results and rewrites the configurations as appropriate.

Take Care When Waiting for Page Elements to Appear

If you are testing a page that makes an Ajax call and you need to wait for it to return before you carry on, then you may be tempted to just sleep for a certain amount of time to give the element a chance to appear. If you do this, though, you can slow down the execution of your test suite by a significant amount if there are several tests that use the same control. Instead, go into a loop with a timeout value and check repeatedly for the element you want until it is present and then click it.

The tighter the loop, the faster the test will run. The exception to this would be if you don't sleep at all, which saturates the CPU and can actually slow things down. If you are going to try this approach with WebDriver, it is worth remembering that WebDriver talks to the browser across the network, so if you are going to repeatedly poll for something, then you can run out of sockets. I found this out when I was busy congratulating myself on speeding up the build just by reducing the sleep time in the wait loop and the tests started failing regularly seemingly at random.

To keep the tests running quickly while not running out of sockets, we implemented a back-off strategy for the sleep time so the first sleep was for 10ms and the second was for 20ms, doubling each time up to a ceiling of two seconds. This worked very well, and the tests remained fast without becoming unreliable.

7.2   Resilient Tests

Resilient tests are tests that don't break when they are not supposed to break. I have seen acceptance test efforts abandoned as a result of a lack of trust in the tests caused by frequent false positives. We call tests that fail when there is no problem with the code under test brittle.

When our tests are brittle, they are less useful. Think of the fable of the boy who cried wolf. If a test fails regularly when the software it is supposed to be testing is not broken, people will quickly begin to ignore it, and as a result, that test is no longer providing any value.

In addition to this, a test that has failed when the system under test is not broken needs to be fixed and is the source of needless work.

So, resilient tests are valuable because the team will trust them and they are cheaper to maintain.

Select Page Elements Individually

By this I mean you should be able to get hold of each element on a page without reference to any other. Some tools allow you to select elements by XPath, which essentially allows you to provide the tool with a set of directions to the element you want.

> Take the third div on the left, the second ul on the right, and the button you want will be three doors down.

Take a look at this example taken from a real website and recorded using the Firefox plug-in Selenium:

```
"//div[@id='show']/div[2]/div[7]/ul/li[2]/a/span[1]"
```

If you rearrange the page, because you want the back button on the other side of the clear button, for example, then the route changes and your test fails. It would be much better if we could just provide an address and have the tool find its own way there regardless of where it actually is.

Another good reason for not using XPath is that different browsers implement XPath slightly differently, so this selector would select a different element in IE than it would in Firefox. This is because IE's numbering begins at 0 rather than 1, as specified by the W3C. This makes a cross-browser test suite more difficult to implement.

Luckily, tools as well as supporting XPath syntax queries almost always provide support for other methods of access as well. In general, to make a web app testable, we want a unique identifier for each element of the page we are going to interact with. Rather handily, IDs have to be unique and can easily be added to any element we might care to interact with.

Things become a little trickier when you have to deal with lists because obviously it isn't an ID if you duplicate it.

On one recent project, we dealt with lists in our tests by having each list wrapped by a div and uniquely identifying that. The application then generated IDs for each element of the list using the wrapping div ID as the base and appending a number for each list item.

Don't feel you always have to use an ID for identification, though, if you can come up with an alternative method that identifies that element uniquely on the page without tying it unnecessarily to the location of other elements on the page.

For example, if you are confident that your CSS has a good structure and the classes on an element are unlikely to change, then you could use an ID for the list and the css class to get elements from the list.

By selecting elements individually, we avoid tying the tests to the layout of the page. Now when pages get changed around or restyled, the only thing that should cause the test to fail is if the functionality itself has changed.

Take Care When Waiting for Page Elements to Appear (Again)

As well as having a big effect on the performance of your tests, how you wait for page elements to appear can have a significant effect on how resilient to unwanted failure they are.

WebDriver, as with most web testing tools, will usually wait until the page has finished loading. When a page makes asynchronous network calls using Ajax, though, the tool cannot know when it has finished loading, so you need to write the code to do it yourself.

The polling technique mentioned in the *Fast Tests* section is a good way to go, because just waiting for a set time makes your tests either brittle or slow. I feel it is important to mention again, though, because in my experience a significant number of false test failures are failing as a result of not waiting for the correct element.

Here is one example of why this can be difficult. Imagine an app that displays the current temperature in whole degrees. It does not update automatically but has a refresh button that sends an Ajax request to retrieve the new value for the temperature.

If when you click the button the temperature display does not change, how do you know if it worked and the temperature is still the same or if it isn't working and has just not updated?

Even as a human being it is difficult to know whether a system like this is working without being able to vary the temperature at the sensor, so how would we know when to stop waiting in an automated test? We can't wait for the temperature element to be present because it is already here, and we can't wait for the value to change because it may remain the same without being broken.

The only way to really know it is working would be to have a method that allowed you to prod the code that generated the temperature readings so that you could simulate a change in temperature.

The same problem occurs when you have constant screen furniture that adorns every page and you are using this to navigate around the site. Let's assume for the purpose of this example that every page has a Back link.

If you click the Back link, what do you wait for? You can't wait for the Back link to appear because it is already there and will return immediately regardless of whether the page has changed. You can't wait for another arbitrary element to appear in the page model because you don't have any context about which page is the previous page. The only thing you can do is to put a wait method on the page class and have your test call it at the appropriate point.

This is an easy thing to get wrong, and each individual system will have its own idiosyncrasies that you will need to deal with. There are some things you can do, though, to make your life easier in this regard. The first is to identify where you are making Ajax calls. Where you are not making Ajax calls, you will not need to wait for anything because the driver will automatically wait for a page refresh. Where you are making Ajax calls, make sure you don't reimplement the waiting functionality every time and make yourself a couple of utility methods.

```
waitUntilPresent(id)
waitUntilGone(id)
```

Use these in your page model and expose a well-named method to the test so that it is obvious when the method should be used. Here's an example:

```
page.waitForCheeseSelectorToDisappear();
page.waitForBiscuitWidgetToBeVisible();
```

If you give some thought to how you wait for elements to appear in your tests, then you can be confident that they will be resilient, and you will not have intermittent problems relating to timing issues.

Make Your Tests Set Up the Test Data They Rely On

This is good because it guarantees the data your test needs is always available when the test runs, so you can fiddle with test data locally or on a test environment with impunity without worrying about breaking automated tests. This relieves you of the need to manually set up or manage test data. The best way to do this is to use the application's own data management code.

Clean the database before the test starts, insert the data you require, and then run the test.

The reason for this is that if you maintain a separate data setup mechanism such as SQL scripts, then when the application data model changes, the associated changes to the database will break the tests. Now you are in the situation where any change to the data model must be done twice: once for the application and once for the tests. We don't care about any changes to the way the data is persisted to support new functionality if the old functionality remains unchanged. If our tests still pass, then the system still has the data it needs and is doing its job.

How exactly you go about making use of the app's data management code is up to you. You might have your tests in the same code base, in which case you can just include the code you need directly from the system itself. If your tests are in a different code base or written in another language, then there may be a certain amount of work required to present an interface your tests can use. The easiest way if you are writing a website is to provide a little web service that will allow you to make HTTP calls from your tool to set up the data. The web service would just call existing data entry methods in the code base.

You may have an application where there is a large amount of data that the system uses but does not modify. In this case, you may want to maintain a separate test database that you upgrade in the same way you would your production database, thus providing some coverage of your database upgrade process as well. DBDeploy is the tool that I have seen used most often for this purpose and seems to work well. Then you just need to write your database cleaner to knock the system back to this known state rather than wiping it clean and building the whole thing from scratch for every test. If you find that you need to set up test data for which support is not present in the application's data layer, then you should consider adding it to the application code base.

Using the application's data model reduces the number of code changes needed and means that the test's data setup relies on the same code as the rest of the application. You will write less code as a result. Any bugs in the data access code will be exposed because the tests will not have the data they are expecting and will fail. Less code means lower cost and more resilient tests because you have eliminated the possibility of the test's view of the data and the application's view of it being out of sync.

Give Integration Points Their Own Tests

When I talk about an integration point, I mean an existing system that our system needs to use in normal operation. An example of this would be companies that do hit tracking where you make a call to the external system as part of every page load. Another example might be when you have a service that provides information about the users of a system that you rely on to authenticate users. If this external system does not work or we do not talk to it in the correct way, then the software we are writing will not work as intended.

Obviously, if we are using real integration points, then there is the possibility of our build breaking through no fault of our own. Although this is annoying, it is a vital piece of information to have, because clearly any problems you have with the external system during development are likely to be evident in production as well.

What we want to do is to make sure that when an integration point goes down, we don't spend time investigating our own system for a bug when the problem is elsewhere. The best way to do this is to have a section of your build that tests your integration points before your acceptance tests run. Because acceptance tests touch more of the system than our unit tests, it can be a little harder to work out exactly what is failing. By testing that integration points are up and returning the information we expect, we make it easy to identify third parties as the cause of failure. We also have the added bonus of removing another way that acceptance tests can fail without our code being broken.

Ideally we would test integration points first and then go on to run our acceptance tests against real integration points. Sometimes, though, this will not be possible. Perhaps the system you will be interfacing with has not been built yet, or perhaps it is under active development and you find your build is spending more time broken than not. In this situation, you will have to substitute your real integration points for stubs. You should still run all your integration tests, because this at least ensures that your code works against the way you assume the final integration points will work and gives you tests you can run against the real points when they become available.

Our goal is to have as few reasons for a test to fail as possible. Ideally, the only thing that should cause a test to fail is if the thing we are trying to test is broken. If we select by ID, we remove layout changes as a source of failure. By reusing the application's data access layer and setting up and tearing down data as part of each test, we remove database changes as a potential source of error. By setting up separate integration tests, we eliminate the possibility of others breaking the build.

Resilient tests are good. They require less maintenance and will be trusted by the team as a good metric of quality because they will fail only when something is broken.

7.3 Maintainable Tests

But making tests resilient is just one way to make them maintainable.

Use a Page Model

If you have several tests that visit the same page to do different things, then you could write your tests to use the URL of the page directly in every one. If you did this, then if the URL changed, you would have to change it in all the tests that use it. Instead, put details of the page under test into a class so they can be reused. This way, when a page detail has changed, you need to make a change in only one place.

The idea behind a page class is that your interactions with the page should provide an intuitive and concise description of what the browser driver will actually do. Here is an extract from the example tests that illustrates what I mean:

BuildingBetterAcceptanceTests/AnthologyAcceptanceTests/src/tests/CuriousDeveloperDave/DeveloperDav¬
eUserJourneys.java

```
TWHomePage homePage =
    (TWHomePage) ApplicationTestEnvironment.getPage(TWHomePage.class);
homePage.visit();

Assert.assertTrue(homePage.Menu().exists());
Assert.assertTrue("Careers link not present",
                  homePage.Menu().CareersLink().exists());

Menu menu = homePage.Menu();

CareersPage careersInfoPage = menu.clickCareersHomeLink();
Assert.assertEquals("href for careers section on menu not correct url",
                    menu.CareersLink().href(), careersInfoPage.url());
```

As you can see, we get our first page from the application test environment, and then all further interaction is done through the pages. We visit the page, make some assertions about it, and then follow one of the links on the page. In this case, we also have a menu class because all pages on the ThoughtWorks site share the same menu, so it makes sense to represent this as a class too.

The page classes themselves have a field that is an instance of something implementing the WebDriver interface. They know the details of the page and use the driver to interact with the browser.

BuildingBetterAcceptanceTests/AnthologyAcceptanceTests/src/pages/TWHomePage.java

```
public void visit() {
    driver.navigate().to(url);
}

public boolean FeatureBannerIsPresent() {
    List l = driver.findElements(By.id("banner-display"));
    return l.size()>0;
}
```

Using a page model makes your tests much easier to maintain because when a page changes, you just need to change the code in one place rather than in every test that uses it.

Give Your Suite a Coherent Structure

When talking about fast tests, I touched on the idea of user journeys. This idea also gives your suite structure. This makes it easy to find the tests for a certain area of functionality and also makes it easier to know where to add new tests. The act of coming up with a user persona that represents a real user of your system helps you determine what is most important and helps you remember what each user journey is.

As you can see from the example code, the basic structure is pages, tests, and utilities. The utilities should include your waiting code and the application test environment. The pages directory contains all of the code related to encapsulating elements of the site such as menus, buttons, and so on, while obviously all the tests are in the tests directory, with each persona having their own package.

By sticking to a consistent structure for your suite and basing tests around user personas, you reduce the amount of time spent on maintenance because you don't spend time hunting through the test suite trying to find where a particular page was tested or trying to work out where to put a new test.

Treat Your Test Code Like Production Code

Our test code supports our application. If we are confident that our tests are a good barometer of quality, then they allow the team to refactor heavily without worrying about introducing new bugs. They also allow the team to focus less on manual regression testing and more on testing the latest version as it is being developed so that the code is right the first time. Attempting to go faster by paying less attention to our test code will lead to brittle tests and a slow test suite. We will spend more time maintaining the suite and realize less value as a result.

For this reason, it is important to apply the same degree of rigor to your tests as you would to the code that will go live. Refactor your test code where appropriate, and remember that writing the tests and the rapid build feedback that this brings will make your life much easier in the future.

On the projects I have worked on recently, we have written the acceptance test first using the page model and used that to drive out the IDs required for the test. We run the test to be sure it fails and implement the code needed to make it pass. When we arrive at a need for a piece of code that has edge cases that need testing, we immediately drop to the unit level to test those edge cases before coming back up to the acceptance test level. In this way, we finish the code and the tests at the same time and are sure they both work as intended.

Don't Tie Yourself to Your Test Tool

I have been on a project where problems with the tool we were using became apparent, and we had been using it directly in the tests. It was too much effort to rewrite all the tests in another tool, so the tests were neglected and eventually thrown away. The longer you have a test suite, the larger it will get, and the larger the investment of time and effort it represents. Also, as time goes on, the likelihood of your wanting to change your test suite goes up as new features are added to the product or the version of the tool you are using becomes deprecated.

In these situations, you want to make it as easy as possible to move from one tool to another. The best way to do this is to write your tests to an interface rather than a concrete implementation. When you come to move tools, you will have to implement an adapter between the interface your tests use and the methods the new tool provides. This will still require a certain amount of work but will be much less effort than rewriting an entire test suite from scratch.

In the examples here, we have been using WebDriver. This is quite a good choice because it is open source, and as you can see in the code, WebDriver is the interface, and then there are different sorts of drivers that implement it: HtmlUnitDriver, FirefoxDriver, and so on. I have found the WebDriver interface very easy and intuitive to use, and because you can download the source, you may as well write your tests against that and write an adapter for whatever tool you move to if you find that the actual implementations provided by WebDriver fail to meet your requirements at some point in the future.

Use a page model, and you will need to make fewer changes to your tests when the application changes. Give your suite a coherent structure and make use of user journeys. This will make it easier to find tests in the suite and make it more obvious where a new test should go. Treat your test code like production code because spending a bit of time on your tests when you write them will save a lot of time in the future. Use a browser driver interface to make it easy to move to a different tool should you need to do so. Your tests will need less time spent on them, and you can spend more effort actually developing your product.

7.4   Making It Work

We have gone through a number of different things you can do to make your tests fast, resilient, and maintainable. Many of the suggestions I have made rely on the developers being closely involved in writing the tests. I suggested using IDs for the page model. It is very difficult to do this if you don't write the tests first and then the code because if you are not writing this sort of test, you won't know exactly which elements to put IDs on. Using the data layer is difficult if you do not have development involvement because the correct methods may not be available or the people writing the tests will not know how to do it or how to reference the correct piece of code.

Some of the other suggestions such as coming up with personas for the users and coming up with the most important user journeys are activities where business analysts and QAs are going to have significant input.

The expertise to implement all these suggestions exists in most teams, so why do acceptance testing efforts sometimes go wrong? I believe the issue is that the task is often given to either a group of developers or a group of testers. The testers without help from the developers are less likely to write maintainable tests, while developers are less likely to structure the suite well or consider the site from the point of view of the end user. It is only when we can bring both groups of people together and write the tests at the same time the code is being written that we can get everybody's input at the right time.

I believe that it is vitally important to have a process that encourages people to collaborate. The following practices are all ones we use and make it possible for us to write our tests in the way I have been describing. There is not enough space here to do them all justice, and they are practices that apply to the whole development effort, but ideally I can at least outline how they contribute to writing good acceptance tests.

Co-location

The team should be structured around a project and the developers, testers, business analysts, and project manager should all sit together around the same desks. They should be close enough so that anyone on the team can ask anyone else a question without needing to move or raise their voice. This means that when someone has a question, it is easier to just ask and have it answered than it is to raise a bug or a ticket and bat it back and forth on some piece of software. This aids communication.

Test Maintenance Is Everybody's Job

It is the responsibility of the QAs to make sure that the tests are well-structured user journeys and that the most important parts of the system are covered. It is the developer's responsibility to make sure that the test suite is well written and maintainable. It is everybody's responsibility to make sure that the tests are being run. It is also everybody's responsibility to be aware of the status of the tests, and if someone breaks a test, then it is their responsibility to fix the application; or if the application is not broken, then it is their responsibility to fix the test and work out why the test failed when the application was not broken.

Story Huddle

When the developers are ready to begin work on a new piece of functionality, the QA, developer, and business analyst should get together to discuss the new functionality and what the acceptance criteria are. This discussion has the following tangible outputs:

- Identify an appropriate user journey to test this functionality and how this test will be extended.

- Identify acceptance criteria against which the finished story will be assessed.

- Identify any areas of uncertainty where additional analysis is required.

The benefit of this is that we clear up any ambiguities in the story before development begins, ensuring that what the business analyst intends and what the developer and QA understand is the same thing. This means fewer bugs will be raised in error, and there will be fewer incorrect interpretations of a written set of requirements. By identifying acceptance criteria together and identifying the user journeys to be modified, we have done the groundwork needed to make sure our acceptance tests will be appropriate and valuable.

Pair on Test Development

When the developer begins development (ideally this should be immediately after the story huddle), they should sit with the QA team to write a failing acceptance test.

The benefit of this is that the developer's input on the structure of the test suite will help ensure the suite is maintainable and the tests are not brittle. The QA's input will ensure that all the agreed criteria are covered by the automated test. There is also the benefit of knowledge sharing between both parties, and the whole team will be satisfied that if the test passes, it actually means something, thus increasing confidence in the tests.

When I wrote the example tests for this article, I had a few problems that would have been resolved if I had been working with the developers to write the tests.

The first problem I had was that not all the elements I wanted to interact with had IDs. This means that to come up with a comprehensive suite of tests after the fact, tests would have to use relative paths to elements to reference elements on the page, making them more brittle. If I had been working with the developers, it would have been a simple matter to come up with a set of unique IDs and have them added to the page to make the acceptance tests more resilient.

The second problem I had was the menu class. If you look at the way I implement it, I instantiate an instance of the appropriate page class and navigate to the correct URL manually. This has the same end result as actually clicking the link on the page, but because it achieves this by relying on knowledge of the correct URL, we lose the ability to test the actual URL in the link to see whether it is the correct one.

The reason I did this was because I wanted the tests to run headless, and the HTMLUnit driver does not support hover while the real browser drivers do. WebDriver is not able to interact with elements that are marked as hidden, so we need to fire the correct event to make the menu visible before WebDriver can interact with it. To test this properly, there are two possible solutions: the first is to lose the ability to run the tests headless and use only real browser drivers. If we were going to take this approach, the ideal implementation would have an ID on the link we want to follow. We would cast our element to a renderable web element that would allow us to expose the hidden menu and interact with it in the page class in the following way:

```
WebElement careersMenu = driver.findElement(By.Id("mainMenu"));
    RenderedWebElement renderableCareersMenu = (RenderedWebElement) careersMenu;
    renderableCareersMenu.hover();
    driver.findElement(By.Id("OurProcess")).click();
```

The second way would be for us to put a hook into our JavaScript code to make testing easier; the hook would fire the correct event to make the menu display. You could then enable JavaScript in the HTMLUnit driver and cast it to a JavaScript executor like so:

```
JavascriptExecutor js = (JavascriptExecutor) driver;
js.executeScript("javascriptMethodCall");
```

Story Demo

When development is complete, the finished feature and acceptance test should be demoed to the business analyst and QA team. All the acceptance criteria should be covered, and the QA team can see that the test they worked on with the developer now passes when previously it failed.

The benefit here is that at this point we have covered all the obvious scenarios as well as having an automated acceptance test. The story can now pass to the QA team to be tested with a good chance of passing without further changes.

7.5 Wrapping Up

I believe that the most important thing to get right to make your acceptance tests work is the process. If you don't write your tests at the same time as your code, you can't follow a lot of the practices I have recommended, and without working together and communicating frequently in a structured manner, such as the story huddle and story demo, you can't get the right input at the right time from the right people.

If you do work like this, though, it will make the technical advice in this article easier to follow. You will end up with a suite of acceptance tests that run quickly, break infrequently, provide a lot of value, and take little effort to maintain.

And ultimately these tests will provide you with an additional safety net for your code and make releasing frequently to production less risky.

Part III

Issues in Software Development

Four ThoughtWorkers tackle a variety of software development topics, from modern Java web applications to driving business innovation into the delivery phase.

CHAPTER 8

Modern Java Web Applications

by Sam Newman

Many if not most Java web applications have followed the tramlines laid down by the HTTP Servlet API and the containers that support them. For years, scale was handled by bigger boxes running multiple threads that were clustered to provide resiliency and increase capacity. Various commercial container vendors touted their ever-growing feature sets, using them as a selling point. In much of the rest of the web development world, though, Java web application design was not looked at favorably. It seemed as though the idiomatic Java web app was developed in a vacuum, taking little account of the successful development done in PHP, Python, Ruby, and so on. A cynic would identify the vendors as behind much of the limited thinking of how Java web applications should be built; in an enterprise world, it is feature richness that sells vendor products, not simplicity (or even in some cases fitness for purpose).

Over the duration of several large-scale web projects, we at ThoughtWorks evolved a more commonsense approach to building highly scalable, highly testable web applications. Borrowing the best ideas from other platforms, I hope to share some of these ideas with the rest of the Java development community. These ideas include the following:

- Stateless application servers
- Segmentation by freshness and progressive enhancement
- Out-of-container testing and containerless web applications
- Post redirect GET

It should be worth noting that while much of this chapter talks about Java web applications, the underlying patterns apply equally to other languages (and in many cases are in widespread use by applications outside of the enterprise Java world).

8.1 The Past

Before we talk about what is different about how we think you should build Java web apps, it is probably worth talking about the traditional, idiomatic Java web application.

Stateful Server

The HTTP Servlet API gave programmers a very convenient way to store data pertaining to a user session, namely, HttpSession. This class allowed us to store all sorts of information—tracking IDs, shopping carts, history, and so on. From a programmer's point of view, this abstraction yielded all sorts of benefits. However, there are two prime downsides with this approach: failover and performance.

The session has to be kept in memory for as long as it is needed by the user. But how long is that? If the user logs out, you can purge the session, but many users don't explicitly log out, and for some cases you'll need to track a session without the user logging in. So, how does the server know when it can get rid of a session? All it can do is wait for a certain period of time after the last user request before purging the session. You can tune this time to try to reduce memory use, but if you keep the session too short, users get frustrated at losing their state. Too long, and you will have memory issues.

Under the hood, the Servlet container is passing around a cookie to identify the user. The session data is not being passed over the wire; instead, the container retrieves the data that matches the cookie. For many people using this mechanism, the first time they encountered a problem with this approach was when they had more than one web server on the back end, with a load balancer in front. Now, the load balancer has to be configured to use sticky sessions, meaning that subsequent requests from the same user go to the same server on the back end.

Enabling sticky sessions on a load balancer is only part of the problem. Now, traffic can be routed back to a node that has the session data. What happens when that node dies, though? Surely we can't be happy to just lose that session. To solve that problem, servlet container vendors developed various clustering solutions. Clustering for session replication does bring additional challenges, however, and we'll address those issues later.

Container Dependence

From very early on, much importance was being placed upon the capabilities provided by the various servlet containers that emerged. These servers would take away much of the pain from us, handling low-level issues such as sockets, main methods, and the like. To write code that ran against the HTTP Servlet API, you had to run in one of these containers—and ideally you avoided calling vendor-specific API calls to ensure your web application maintained portability. For the most part, applications that used only the Servlet API maintain their portability between different containers, but the need for a container remains for most people creating Java web applications.

But for operations departments used to supporting other types of applications, the servlet containers are yet another piece of infrastructure to get their heads around. They already have to understand the behavior of your application, and with a container in the picture, they have to understand how to support and monitor your application as well.

The HTTP Spec Is the Enemy!

Early on, web application developers found that the APIs provided by Sun and implemented by the container were overly verbose and harder to work with than they would like. Predictably enough, a succession of frameworks emerged that attempted to hide these APIs from the end user, instead presenting alternative APIs that would ideally be easier for developers to work with. Open source projects like Struts and WebWork had become very popular, and subsequent frameworks have attempted to provide different ways of building web applications. The problem is that partly because of how some of these frameworks were implemented, end developers remain unaware of how the Web—or more specifically HTTP—actually works. By hiding behind these APIs and deferring decisions to framework authors about what and how parts of HTTP would be supported, a vast number of developers in this space helped create a wide variety of badly behaved (in an HTTP sense) applications.

The standard, badly behaved Java application doesn't set cache headers correctly, uses POSTs for odd things, and rarely sends a 500 response code for an error.

The comparison of many of the popular Java frameworks with more modern HTTP-aware platforms like Webmachine[1] (where it is impossible to create an application that isn't compliant with the HTTP specification) is stark.

Understanding the HTTP specification is important for any web developer and essential for modern web applications. Patterns like Post Redirect GET and Segmentation by Freshness help us create well-behaved applications that solve common problems for web applications.

---

1. https://bitbucket.org/justin/webmachine/wiki/Home

8.2   Stateless Server

Stateless server is one group of techniques.

Clustering

As mentioned earlier, clustering is a feature provided by most servlet containers that allows for data such as session data to be replicated between application nodes so that if one node goes down, data loss is kept to a minimum.

With clustering, user session state is replicated between two or more nodes within each cluster. Because there may be a delay in replication, you still want sticky session load balancing, but at least if the original node fails, the user should get redirected to a node with their session data. Setting up clustering is not hugely complex, but nor is it trivially simple—and typically it is not something developers will have running on their development machines. That means issues like trying to distributed nonserializable sessions between nodes often get picked up late.

Potentially more concerning than the setup cost is the overhead of distributing the whole session between all nodes in the cluster. This can lead to a negative network effect; replication of large session objects has completely saturated internal network links, resulting in site outage more than once. This network effect makes it harder and harder to add nodes to scale out, and clustering across data centers is impractical enough that a data center failover will typically result in the loss of user session. You can start to understand why Mike Nygard states in *Release It! [Nyg07]* that "sessions are the Achilles heel of web applications."

Vendors with distributed caching systems like Gemfire and Terracotta have been pushing them as a more effective means of replicating session state than the standard mechanisms offered for clustering servlet containers. Although there can be many good uses for distributed caches and some of them are excellent products, using them in an attempt to work around problems with traditional session replication is fixing the wrong problem. Dealing with cache invalidation is hard, and the more places in which data is cached, the more complexity there is in understanding how to invalidate data. If you need a distributed cache just to allow for replication of sessions, you may want to give serious thought to simply avoiding the need for session data to be stored on the server in the first place.

Cookies to the Rescue

Anyone who has had to create a web application capable of authenticating a user and creating a session will have had to create a cookie. Whether you did it by hand or handed the task off to your web framework, under the hood a cookie gets created, letting the application server know "this person has logged in." Traditionally, servlet containers would just drop a cookie with an ID when you created an HTTPSession. When retrieving the session state for subsequent requests, the ID in the cookie is used to look up the servlet container's session store.

Rather than just use a cookie to store an ID, we can instead take all kinds of information regarding the session state and put it in the cookie too. With a little thought, we can take the session data we care about and put it in the cookie instead of relying on server-side state that then requires replication.

With the session state in the request, the need for subsequent requests to go to a specific machine is gone. If the last node you hit is down and your next request goes to another machine in the data center (or even fails over to a different data center), you won't notice. This removes the need for sticky sessions on the load balancer and removes much of the need for clustering application servers.

Many sites that deal in massive scale use cookies for session state as a matter of course. This is because for them, the ability to scale application servers in a near-linear fashion is key. The complexity in using a cookie for session state is minor compared to the complexity in managing data replication on the server side. If you can do without the clustering of application servers, failover becomes simpler, scaling becomes easier, and you may also save money if you no longer have to shop around for servlet containers with "Now with improved clustering support!" slapped on the box.

Ever wondered how all those systems written in PHP scaled to millions of users using nothing but Apache (and not a clustering container in sight)? Well, now you know part of the reason why.

Separating User-Specific Data

One of the first things to understand is that even though they are small, cookies can add up. If you drop a cookie for the www.mycompany.com domain, a user agent will send a cookie for all requests to that domain. That will include requests that probably don't care about the exact state of the user's session (and perhaps not even that they are an authenticated user), such as static imagery or CSS files. If possible, segment your traffic and drop session state cookies only for those subdomains that need session state; for example, you may not need to send any cookies for static.mycompany.com but will need one for myapp.mycompany.com.

Secure Cookies

When making the move to put session state in a user cookie, understand how that cookie can be used. What would happen if that cookie was captured by some unscrupulous person? It is not as theoretical a risk as you might think; every time you use HTTP over an unsecured wireless network (consider airport lounges or coffee shops), other people can grab your cookies. If an individual makes their own requests with your cookie, they have the potential to "steal" your session. In fact, the Firesheep[2] Firefox extension was developed for the very purpose of showing you how serious and real a problem this is; it allows you to browse all the cookies being sent over the local network.

One way to avoid this is sending all data over HTTPS, but HTTPS traffic does have an increased overhead, not only on the client and server in terms of processing time but also in terms of an overhead in bandwidth. On a large-scale site, this bandwidth overhead can be significant—significant enough that you want to limit the use of HTTPS to only the data that needs the additional level of protection.

One answer is to send only session state over HTTPS and send all other traffic over HTTP. When authenticating a user, drop a cookie during authentication using the Secure[3] attribute. This ensures that user agents will send the cookie only over HTTPS, and it cannot therefore be stolen.

However, what if you want to surface some content specifically for the user over HTTP—content that, if hijacked, represents a minimal security risk—but want to send more secure content over HTTPS? As before, access to the really secure content needs a Secure cookie that is sent only over HTTPS, but less secure user-specific content just needs a standard, nonsecure cookie that gets sent over HTTP. All you then need to do is drop both types of cookies during your authentication process.

To consider a real-world example, imagine a shopping site. The HTTP cookie gets dropped and may have a long time to live (potentially several weeks). The presence of this cookie allows the site to surface personal recommendations to you and the near de facto standard "Welcome, Joe Blogs!" message. But when you come to check your order, you can't afford for someone else to

---

2.   http://codebutler.com/firesheep
3.   http://tools.ietf.org/html/rfc6265#section-4.1.2.5

pretend to be you, so we need to check for the presence of the secure cookie and route you over HTTPS. This secure cookie can have a much shorter time to live, reducing the exposure to people accessing the cookie by accessing the machine itself. If the secure cookie doesn't exist, you may be asked to log in again (over HTTPS, of course). So, the worst case is someone could grab your shopping basket, but they couldn't check it out or access your billing information.

8.3   Container Considered Optional

While containers can provide potentially useful features such as clustering, monitoring, and control, these features may provide little benefit when developing our code. The very presence of the container seems to hinder developing and testing our applications. Without container-specific hot-deployment technology, feedback cycles can be long enough to really impact a team's productivity, and some containers are often nontrivial to install and automate as part of a continuous integration build. In addition, if the only way to run tests that give enough confidence is to stand up an entire server stack, our build times will be quite long too.

Out-of-Container Testing

Python's WSGI API was inspired by the Servlet API,[4] but unlike Java it has a viable mock layer for the API in the form of wsgi_intercept[5] that allows tests to be run against a mock HTTP transport. This results in significantly reduced test times. By implementing our application against an API that can be run inside or outside a servlet container, we will have many of the benefits in Java that Python web programmers already have because of wsgi_intercept.

At this point, it is probably worth a brief diversion to talk about testing. Generally speaking, you need to balance the types of automated tests you write. Mike Cohn has a nice model for this, with the different types of tests mapped to a pyramid (Figure 7, *Mike Cohn's testing pyramid*, on page 150). Variations of Mike's pyramid show the different levels as variously unit/service/UI, unit tests/acceptance tests/GUI tests, and the like, but the best variation I have seen has each layer representing tests that cover increasing levels of scope, so in our example, we show small, medium, and large-scoped tests.

---

4.   http://www.python.org/dev/peps/pep-0333/
5.   http://code.google.com/p/wsgi-intercept/

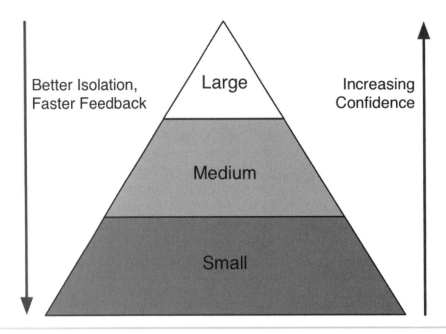

Figure 7—Mike Cohn's testing pyramid

Different projects tend to have different names for their tests, but the same principles apply. Those tests at the bottom of the pyramid represent small-scoped tests. These are the kinds of tests you'll be creating when using Test-Driven Design (something we do as a matter of course at ThoughtWorks). These small-scoped tests typically test only a very small amount of functionality—perhaps a single method. These tests are fast, and when they fail, you tend to know with a good degree of precision what has broken. However, by their very nature, each one tests only a fraction of the overall system, so one test passing does not give you a high degree of confidence that the system works as intended.

As you go further up the pyramid, you have tests that cover larger amounts of scope. In the web development world, those tests at the top of the pyramid will execute the end-to-end behavior of the system, typically using some driver technology like Selenium or Watir. As you might expect, when these tests pass, we get a higher degree of confidence that the system works as intended.

One of the downsides with these large-scoped tests is that they take a long time to run for a number of reasons. Often the problem with speed is that real browsers are being used to drive the test. For example, consider this canonical example using the WebDriver API from Selenium 2 being used to search for *Modern Java Web Applications* using Firefox:

```
WebDriver driver = new FirefoxDriver();
driver.navigate().to("http://www.google.com");

WebElement element = driver.findElement(By.name("q"));
element.sendKeys("Modern Java Web Applications!");
element.submit();
```

In the previous example, a real browser will be launched and used to drive the test. But do we really need a real browser at all? Are we testing complex, browser-specific behavior? Selenium 2 does provide an HTMLUnit abstraction that runs the test in a fake browser, using Rhino to simulate the browser's JavaScript execution. Rhino has come a long way and can support pretty complex JavaScript applications built using things like JQuery. And all we have to do to avoid the browser tax? Replace new FirefoxDriver() with new HtmlUnit-Driver(). In general, try to avoid the need for too many in-browser tests, and consider making use of fake browsers for testing the default.

Another thing that can cause slow browser tests is the need to connect over a socket in the first place. If we remove the need for a real browser, can we remove this requirement too? Unfortunately, all WebDriver implementations currently assume that you are connecting to a remote URL, which requires that the endpoint you are testing is available on a socket somewhere. To try to get around this limitation, Alex Harin and other ThoughtWorks colleagues created Inproctester.[6] This allows you to still write tests at the level of the WebDriver API, but instead of expecting to reach out over sockets, you talk directly to the underlying API of an embedded servlet container; currently both SimpleWeb and Jetty are supported.

The beauty of this? If you decide you actually want to run the same test against a running container using a real browser, you just launch the container and swap in a different WebDriver implementation in your tests.

The result? In practice, we get a significant order-of-magnitude improvement in test times. The exact time savings will depend on what the tests are doing, but in one project, we typically expected our container tests to run in a fraction of a second, and we could run more than a thousand in less than four minutes on a standard desktop machine. One final note before we move on—none of this is really new. Python programmers were doing exactly the same thing

---

6. See https://github.com/aharin/inproctester and the related .NET library Plasma by Jennifer Smith and other ThoughtWorkers that actually predates Inproctester (https://github.com/jennifersmith/plasma).

using WSGI and Twill for testing Python applications many years ago, but efforts to do something similar in Java and .NET web stacks seemed much thinner on the ground until now.

Do You Need a Container at All?

So, we've established that you can successfully build a web application in a stateless manner, which completely sidesteps the need for clustering. You can run all of your tests outside the container for high-speed testing. So, do you even need a container? Well, in many cases the answer is no—some lightweight (but still HttpServlet API–compliant) containers can also be run in an embedded mode, like Jetty. Rather than deploying an application as a WAR file inside an already running container, you instead can just run a main method that launches the lightweight web server for your application. These applications don't require commercial licenses and typically run just as fast as their container-bound versions.

When running an embedded container, there is no need for a web.xml, WAR file structure, or anything else. If you wanted, you could wire up the entire application using code. You could use onejar[7] to bundle your entire application server into an executable JAR file; then just run java -jar myapp.war, and up comes your application server.

Running web applications without a container can often result in a much simpler deployment approach, and unless you rely extensively on features provided by servlet containers, I strongly suggest you look at running without one.

8.4 Segmentation by Freshness

Segmentation by Freshness is another group of techniques.

Caching: The Secret Sauce Behind Scaling Websites

We had a question on our internal mailing lists recently—"What servlet container would you use for a massively scalable web-based system?" The answer I almost (glibly) posted was "One that doesn't get hit." If our application container needs to do less work—handle fewer requests—we need to worry less about needing to throw faster containers, bigger machines, or more machines at the problem. The answer to not getting hit in the first place? Caching.

In any web application that gets viewed by real people, you already have at least one cache that can take the burden from your site—the browser cache.

---

7.   http://one-jar.sourceforge.net/

This cache (ideally) obeys the information placed in headers regarding how often it should check for updates to content it already has. Even once the browser decides to check for content again, it can issue a conditional GET; if your site can correctly issue a 304 Not Modified response (remember: know your HTTP spec), then the browser can still use the locally cached version.

The reality is that there will probably be other caches between browsers and the website. You may be employing content delivery networks like CloudFront or Akamai. Your ISP may be caching, as may corporate networks. Or you may be taking advantage of Squid, Varnish, or Nginx as reverse proxies. The nice thing about setting the right cache headers is that you can take advantage of all of these systems almost for free.

Knowing What to Cache

Let's start a simple example. Imagine an article on a news site. The bulk of the content represents very static content—site furniture such as CSS, JavaScript, images that will probably change only between releases, and the article itself that may change only a few times for minor edits. However, the modern new website will contain a plethora of more dynamic, often user-targeted content: a list of the five most recently published articles, for example; snippets of recent breaking news; or offers targeted at a logged-in individual.

We want to use caching to reduce how often people request this page from the server. Site furniture will be loaded from separate requests, so they can use long-lived cache headers. However, what about the HTML itself, with a mix of fairly static content (the article) and content that we need to be fresh? We could set the cache header to be short enough such that we ensure the freshness of the more dynamic content, but then we are still pulling back a large amount of content that has not changed.

So, how do we ensure that we can have a long time to live for static content but ensure we get fresh content? Segmentation by Freshness[8] is the answer.

Introducing Segmentation by Freshness

Segmentation by Freshness is the process by which a page is split into a series of fragments, which are then assembled to produce the final page. Each fragment is segmented based on how fresh the content needs to be. So, in

8. Martin Fowler originally documented this pattern after it was used extensively on two large-scale web projects at ThoughtWorks, but like all patterns, it certainly was in widespread use prior to this: http://martinfowler.com/bliki/SegmentationByFreshness.html.

our news example, we may have two fragments: the article and the "most viewed articles" widget.

These segments can be aggregated into the final page on the server side or on the client side. With server-side aggregation (Figure 8, *Server-side aggregation of content*, on page 154), one request can result in multiple fragments being retrieved—some from caches and some from the server itself—before the final page is returned over the wire to the user's browser. You can reuse existing reverse proxies in your infrastructure to act as fragment caches for your pages.

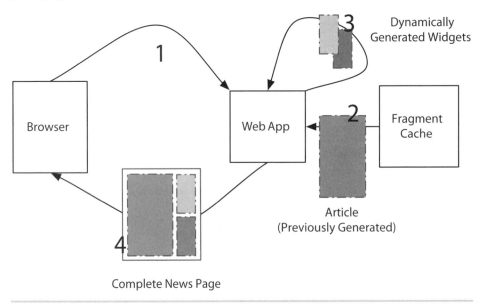

Figure 8—Server-side aggregation of content

One downside with this approach is that ideally we'd like the client to fetch the article body from their local browser cache and fetch only the latest, most popular widget content from the server; as it is, we have to route the traffic for both from the server. Client-side aggregation (Figure 9, *Client-side aggregation of content*, on page 155) is an alternative approach that can be used to solve this problem. With client-side aggregation, an HTML page is sent to the client with a series of JavaScript payloads that then reach out from the browser to pull in additional content. The browser just issues GETs for the various fragments it needs; as long as those GET responses provide proper cache headers, then the browser can use locally cached versions.

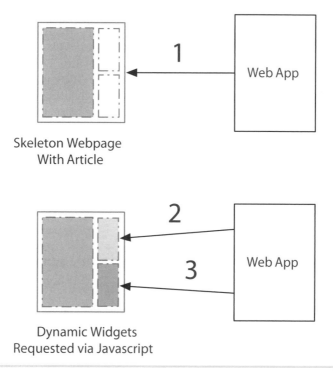

Figure 9—Client-side aggregation of content

One potential downside to client-side aggregation is that JavaScript (or some similar client-side technology) is required. With enough of the page being stitched together using client-side technology, the burden being placed on the client can cause a performance issue. Older machines/browsers will struggle to execute a lot of JavaScript, leading to the page appearing to load slowly (with boxes being "painted in"), even if your system on the server side is happily handling the load. Another downside is that parts of your page that are constructed by JavaScript will not be visible to search engines; however, if you ensure that the content you want to surface to search engines is returned in the initial static HTML payload, you'll still get the search traffic you want.

Because of the various pros and cons of the two aggregation approaches, you may need to use a mix of both techniques. Factors that will influence the right approach include the location of the users, the browsers they use, and the types of computer they have, so you may need to tweak things to find the exact balance for you.

Progressive Enhancement

The method of assembling a web page using JavaScript calls (client-side aggregation) is helpful in implementing progressive enhancement. When trying to support multiple types of user agent, you have to work out how to deal with different capabilities. Some sites choose to implement two (or more) sets of pages: one for fully featured browsers and others for more basic browsers like IE6 or screen reader devices. Steven Champeon[a] coined the term *progressive enhancement* (also known as *graceful degradation*) for those sites that choose instead to initially load a basic HTML page and then execute JavaScript calls to decorate the HTML with more advanced UI features, richer content, and so on. The more basic browsers do not execute the JavaScript to enhance the page and therefore never see code they cannot execute. The key is that the basic HTML page is capable of letting users use the core features of the site; for example, on a shopping site, they can still check out.

---

a.   For more background, see http://www.hesketh.com/thought-leadership/our-publications/progressive-enhancement-and-future-web-design.

A Brief Introduction to Reverse Proxies and Content Delivery Networks

Both reverse proxies like Varnish and Squid and content delivery networks (CDNs) like CloudFront or Akamai sit in front of your website. In their simplest configurations, they obey cache headers on content and store HTTP responses in fast, optimized caches—typically in memory. All requests pass through these types of caches, and the request is routed to the underlying web application only if the content is not present in the cache or it has expired.

CDNs differ from reverse proxies in two key ways. First, they are typically provided by third parties and are hosted by machines distributed across the world, whereas reverse proxies typically sit in the same data centers as the underlying application server. Second, CDNs use DNS lookups to ensure that traffic is routed to cache nodes near the originating request. For example, if the server hosting the website I am using is based in the United States but it is fronted by a CDN with nodes near me in the United Kingdom, I may well find cached content being served in a faster, lower-latency fashion from a service in my own country.

When choosing between a reverse proxy or a CDN, the prime considerations are price and user location. Varnish, Squid, and Nginx are all available for free (although you'll need your own hardware), whereas CDNs are a commercial offering, with a fee typically based on the amount of bandwidth used. If your user base is geographically distributed close to your own data centers, you may not get any benefit from a CDN. On the other hand, a global user base may well have you looking at the more advanced capabilities of a managed CDN solution.

Both reverse proxies and CDNs allow you varying degrees of configuration. Some people are tempted to configure caching rules in the cache itself, rather than simply serving the right headers from the application in the first place. I strongly advise against configuring the time to live for content in these caches. First, as mentioned, there are other types of caches that are present on the network that can benefit from headers set in your application. Second, by keeping the cache behavior in your application, you allow yourself to switch in different reverse proxies or CDNs with minimal changes.

8.5 Post Redirect GET

A common problem in developing any applications that accept data via a POST is handling duplicate requests. To see how this can be an issue, let's consider a simple example.

Example: A Shopping Cart

A user navigates around a site, adding an item from time to time to the shopping basket. At the end, they click the Buy Now button on the cart. This initiates a POST to the server: the contents of the shopping cart are stored in the POST parameters. Once the purchase is processed on the server side, a receipt is rendered to the user in the response of the POST.

The user bookmarks the resulting receipt. Later, the user goes back to the bookmark only to find the receipt gone. Why?

The problem with this scenario is that when bookmarking a page, you bookmark only the URI, not the POST parameters. You don't actually want to bookmark the parameters, of course; otherwise, when you revisited a bookmark, you could (depending on the application design) end up resubmitting your order again. What you do want, though, is to see your receipt.

Likewise, how often have you clicked Refresh only to be asked if you want to resubmit the form parameters? And if you did that, what would you expect? Does it make sense for a user to send the same request twice?

The Post Redirect GET pattern[9] attempts to sidestep these issues. Once the server has processed the POST, rather than rendering the response back (for example, the receipt in the previous example), it instead sends a redirect to

---

9. See page 36 of *Universal Design for Web Applications [CM08]* by Wendy Chisholm and Matt May for details (O'Reilly Media, 2008).

the browser telling it where to fetch the result. The browser then initiates a GET for the resulting redirect (Figure 10, *Example post redirect GET*, on page 158).

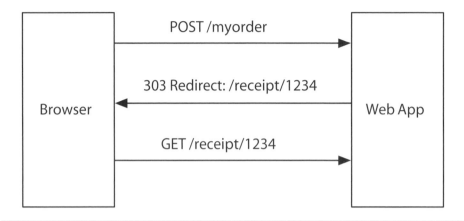

POST /myorder

303 Redirect: /receipt/1234

Browser

GET /receipt/1234

Web App

Figure 10—Example post redirect GET

The resource the browser is redirected to can then be refreshed or bookmarked without any of the concerns outlined earlier.

One additional benefit of this approach comes when considering potentially long workflows. Each step can return the manipulated state via a GET that can be bookmarked, and the workflow can be picked up again at some midway point (assuming the application is designed to allow for this).

A Brief Note About Response Codes

According to the HTTP 1.1 spec,[a] the correct redirect to send in the example of a post redirect GET is a 303 See Other. A 303 tells the browser (or any other user agent) that the response is found under a different URI and that a GET should be performed to retrieve the response at the given URI. In this situation, many applications use a 302, which under HTTP 1.0 was classified as Moved Temporarily and which most browsers interpret the same as a 303. 303 was introduced in the HTTP 1.1 spec to disambiguate some implementations for handling 302s, but that is a longer discussion for another place.

---

a.   See http://tools.ietf.org/html/rfc2616#page-63.

8.6   Wrapping Up

As we have seen, multiple different techniques are available when building Java web applications that fall outside the standard approaches. These techniques in our experience yield significant improvements, in terms of usability of the final system, developer productivity, lower software costs, and reduced operational overhead.

Many of the techniques outlined in this chapter can be used on their own or together. The important thing is to realize that the standard, vendor way of doing things isn't already the best. By the time this book is published, it is highly probable that smart people around the world may have come up with all sorts of interesting improvements in this space—it is up to you to find them, and experiment, to work out what is best for you.

CHAPTER 9

Taming the Integration Problem

by Julio Maia

When you do incremental interactive development, every integration point poses a challenge. When a system embodies many integration points, you face a whole series of challenges.

Ideally, you want to test any change in the system against the integration environment. Practically, you often can't, since integration problems can be unstable, data-changing, slow, or even nonexistent.

So, you are forced to test against a stand-alone environment for quick feedback. Although this will not be sufficient to validate the system, *done right*, it can be used to quickly identify problems in the system in an integrated fashion and to isolate problems with the actual integration environment.

You need to isolate concerns and define contracts related to integration points. Doing so requires careful modularization and comprehensive testing strategies.

But although standard modularization and componentization techniques can be used to deal with separation of concerns, they may not be sufficient. It's crucial to define executable contracts through testing and enforce that implementation details from subsystems don't contaminate the main integration system.

Testing can be seen as an example of *agreement media* across different stakeholders and teams regarding the expected behaviors of the system and its integration points.

You want to create and maintain testing infrastructure and the implementation of modularization approaches that support decentralized and efficient delivery. You will experience obstacles, because nontechnical stakeholders will be constantly tempted to set low priorities for units of work that they do not perceive as directly related to features.

Rather than butt heads, here's where it's important to increase visibility about the productivity gains achieved by focusing on quick feedback and educating all stakeholders on the importance of developing and maintaining the required infrastructure.

You increase visibility by collecting metrics, so it's important to see collecting metrics as a proper development activity.

9.1 The Continuous Integration Approach

Some classes of tests have to be run against proper integration environments in order to validate system features. Examples of such tests are integration tests, functional/acceptance tests, and performance tests. In practice, those environments have a combination of the following characteristics:

- *They are unstable*: Their uptime is not guaranteed, or they may suffer from performance or behavior variances that can cause random timeouts and inconsistent responses.

- *They are slow*: Their response time is not fast enough to accommodate the demands of automated testing; build scalability may demand more processing power than what integration servers provide.

- *They are not always available*: They may not be running all the time, because the resources required to provide their services are too expensive or available only during specific times.

- *Their data is changing frequently*: For any number of reasons, the data required for testing may be changing, and the cost of avoiding that may be prohibitive.

- *They may not even exist*: Teams may be working concurrently to build a solution that will be integrated at a later stage.

In those cases, Continuous Integration can be seriously impaired. Because tests would be frequently broken and their ability to pass won't be completely dependent on the changes performed to the system, chasing problems may be difficult.

The problems that these types of environments pose to testing can be significant, but they can be mitigated. To do this, we need a *stability reference* to allow for the following:

- Quick and scalable local builds

- Creating a reference for the data that tests expect from the integration environment

- Proving that the system works with reference data

- Pinpointing quickly what are the causes of failure for broken tests in the integration environment

The stability reference environment requires an extra stage for the build pipeline, which is completely stand-alone because it doesn't depend on any external environment.

The Stability Reference

The following implementation approaches can be used to allow for integration and function testing outside the actual integration environment:

- Using test doubles, which implement the same programmatic interfaces as actual components in the system but do not talk with external integration points. For example, a DAO may be reimplemented to provide static data and never talk with a real database.

- Using servers that provide the same data, behavior, and protocols as the actual servers in the integration environment. These servers may or may not be testing fakes, because they may be suitable for production (for example, local deployments of the same servers used in the actual integration environment).

So, how do these approaches stack up?

Test doubles require the creation of artifacts that contain embedded test code. This is not desirable, because it adds complexity to the build process and moves the build pipeline away from a single-artifact discipline. Also, by not exercising the stack required to interact with external systems, test doubles add very limited value for integration and functional testing.

Servers that provide the same behavior and protocols as the actual integration environment are preferable for the stability reference. They may require the creation of custom software in order to replicate the same semantics as the integration servers, but they have the advantage of exercising the whole integration stack and do not require testing code to be built into artifacts (which is a good practice for build pipelines and testing in general).

Integration Stubs

An effective way to prove that a system integrates correctly without building full replicas of the integration points is to create stubs that *impersonate* each integration point. The idea here is that you'd create servers that would behave exactly like the real ones do, although only for the text fixtures used by the integration tests.

Integration stubs provide the same data, protocol, and semantics as their integration environment counterparts. Stand-alone environments are comprised exclusively of stubs and do not depend on external servers. Stubs may or may not run in the application space, but they must be externalized from the application code.

Integration stubs can be implemented using one of the following strategies:

- Local deployments of the same software used in the integration environment or a slimmed-down version of that software (for example, using Oracle express to impersonate an Oracle database).

- Protocol-compatible stock servers (for example, in-memory databases, SMTP servers, FTP servers, and so on)

- Homegrown servers, which can use a number of strategies to acquire data.

  - *Record-and-replay*: Using recording proxies or hooks into the application to create data flow snapshots as tests run over the integration environment (for example, record/replay proxies).

  - *Fixed data*: Using a handcrafted test fixture, made by querying integration servers or otherwise.

  - *Rules reimplementation*: Implementing rules to comply exactly with the semantics of the integration servers. A specific case of this is generators, which provide data using a known sequence.

How do these implementation strategies stack up?

Local deployments of production-compatible servers are sometimes convenient, but they require developers to install and configure servers in their machines (or depend on a single development sever, which imposes a single point of failure) in order to perform changes to the system. This may or may not be a problem, depending on the installation complexity and the number of resources required to have those server performing well enough for testing. They do have the advantage of providing compatibility out of the box.

Protocol-compatible stock servers generally run in memory and perform well but may have compatibility problems that are hard to predict at the beginning of the development process. They are usually chosen to be used as in-memory servers, which do not require local installations.

Homegrown servers may be challenging to build or set up. They are usually not too complicated for read-only systems. However, transactional systems require state management, which in turn requires a careful strategy to differentiate and record transaction data. On the other hand, they are in full control of the developers and are generally built to be lightweight.

Whatever implementation you select, an important directive for creating stand-alone environments is that all stubs need to have their own integration tests. This is necessary in order to guarantee that they behave as expected and to remove the possibility that a major flaw in their implementations would cause the main application code to fail.

The Build Pipeline

If you are able to guarantee that you can test consistently against integration environments, you should perform local builds against the stand-alone environment only. You should attempt to run all integration tests against it, instead of resorting to subsets of the full test suite and rely on CI servers to run all tests, which inevitably will render your builds broken frequently. For systems with a large number of tests, running all tests in local builds may be impractical without using parallelization. The use of lightweight, in-memory stubs allow for the distribution of tests across different machines, enabling build scalability.

If you implement the impersonated environment properly, builds against that environment should never break. This means there is no excuse to ever have builds in the pipeline associated with a broken stand-alone environment.

If you do this, testing against the actual integration environment is something that can be safely deferred to later stages in the pipeline. Then if tests are found to be broken there, one of the following possibilities should apply:

- The stubs do not provide the same protocol and semantics as the integration servers.

- Data has changed in the integration servers.

- The integration servers were not available or didn't perform consistently.

Most of your broken builds will probably be because of reasons 2 and 3. The stability reference provides the ability to pinpoint most problems in the application code when running in an integrated fashion, but it's not able to identify problems with the integration environment. This means there's still the need for something to help isolate problems with the actual integration environment.

The Monitors

Monitors for the integration points used by the build pipeline are processes that continuously collect and display data about the status of those integration points. They are essential to understand if problems in the integration stages of the build pipeline are related to changes in the software, because of problems with the stubs or because of problems with the integration points.

Two types of monitors are essential to disambiguate problems that may happen in the build pipeline.

- *Verify monitor*: To check whether the data provided by the stubs matches the data provided by the integration servers, you should implement a verify feature in each stub. This feature would use the data recorded or stored by the stub to send messages to the real integration point and check whether the data returned matches the response data the stub would return.

- *Availability (or heartbeat) monitor*: You can put another set of monitors in place to check whether the integration environment is available and responsive. They can work by sending a simple reference query to each integration point and measuring response times (or the event of no response at all). These monitors are usually the same used to monitor the production environment.

These monitors can also be used to measure the impact of downtimes and data changes in the delivery throughput. This is particularly useful to drive the prioritization of fixes to the integration points by giving hard data to business stakeholders on the cost of dealing with problems with external systems.

9.2 Defining Integration Contracts

As discussed in the previous sections, dealing with integration points requires a careful approach in building infrastructure to improve visibility and cycle times throughout the development and support life cycles. At the same time, managing interactions across different delivery teams can be challenging.

Isolating concerns across different systems helps create a manageable environment. Shared components can also help minimize the integration complexity. These techniques, however, don't help in maintaining a contract that can be continuously validated and well understood by all stakeholders (technical or nontechnical).

One way to define the expectations across different systems and to increase the visibility about the current status of the system working in an integrated manner is to establish *executable contracts* between systems.

It's not unusual to find integration tests being used to validate the implementation of integration components and being written only for the use of the development team only. Although this practice provides value in continuously validating whether some expectations around integration points are met, it falls short of providing means for external teams to verify whether expectations around their systems are *valid* and to indicate to nontechnical stakeholders the current status of the delivery.

Executable contracts can be defined by writing integration tests as acceptance tests with narratives that can be understood by different teams. Because those tests run in the Continuous Integration environment, their reports can be used to track the status for each integration point.

9.3 Metrics and Visibility

Several problems related to integration can cause slowdowns and increased costs to a project. It may not be straightforward to track those problems and understand what has to be addressed in order to maximize the throughput in the project.

To help prioritize the solutions to problems regarding integration with external systems, here are some metrics you might want to capture:

- Number of builds broken when run against the integration environment
- Which features of the system are usually broken because of integration problems
- Availability and response times for each integration point
- How frequently data used by tests changes in the integration environment
- The cost of dealing with different types of problems with integration points

It's important to produce those metrics continuously, as opposed to a one-off manually driven activity. The effort required to add automation in order to produce metrics like those is usually small, which justifies the investment in building a dashboard that correlates data and increases the visibly on the impact that dealing with integration points causes to the project.

9.4   Wrapping Up

It's unfortunate that a large number of projects suffer with problems related to integrating with other systems to the point that most changes to it become too risky and too expensive, therefore impacting the ability of implementing features incrementally with short feedback cycles.

The cost of dealing with integration points is usually small when projects start, and little attention is given to building infrastructure for testing and monitoring to support development. As the system incrementally requires more integration points, the number of problems related to dealing with external systems increases rapidly and can seriously impact the ability to add new features to the system safely.

It seems to be the case that nontechnical stakeholders don't prioritize fixes to problems related to integration mostly because they don't understand the extent of the impact that integration problems cause. Technical stakeholders, on the other hand, do understand the nature of the problem, but it's not unusual to observe the situation in which they're pressed to deliver features while not addressing the root causes for the always increasing slowdowns caused by integration problems.

Although it's nontrivial to deliver systems that require complex integrations with external systems, it's not too hard to minimize the problem and create a sustainable and manageable development environment, but that doesn't come without constant effort. It is necessary to continuously build testing infrastructure to allow for quick feedback on changes to the system while increasing visibility on the precise problems that integrating with external systems may be causing to the development process. At the same time, it's fundamental that the contracts with different teams can be validated automatically as the system is being built. Ultimately, focus on creating infrastructure that enables developers and the business to understand and prioritize what is necessary to continuously improve on the software delivery, without creating a never-addressed technical debt backlog.

CHAPTER 10

Feature Toggles in Practice

by Cosmin Stejerean

One of the common ways of working on multiple features concurrently is to use version control branches to develop features in isolation and to merge each feature back into the main line when the work is complete. This is the Feature Branch[1] pattern.

The problem with this approach is that branches of code developed in isolation do not get integrated for a long time and therefore avoid the benefits of Continuous Integration.[2] The longer the branch is separated from the main line, the more risk accumulates from delaying the integration. This usually becomes apparent when trying to merge the branch back into the main line. Does merging a couple of months of work sound like fun?

The naïve solution to dealing with complicated merges in long-running branches is to merge changes in the main line into the feature branch on a regular basis. This approach, however, can go only so far. Developers working in the main line have little or no visibility into the work happening in the feature branch. Refactorings performed in the main line will have to be manually merged into the feature branches, even if those refactorings were often performed without taking into account the work in the feature branch.

Refactorings performed by the developers working in the feature branch will only complicate future merges and can lead to situations where it takes longer to merge a unit of work than it took to develop it originally. This leads to an aversion to making changes that would introduce complicated merge conflicts. Necessary refactorings are postponed or avoided entirely. Technical debt goes through the roof.

---

1. http://martinfowler.com/bliki/FeatureBranch.html
2. http://www.martinfowler.com/articles/continuousIntegration.html

Another approach that has been gathering some attention recently is to develop all features of the application in the main line. This approach is also known as *trunk-based development*.[3] It works great when work on all of the in-progress features can be completed within a single release cycle. When completing all features within a single release cycle is not possible, incomplete features must be *turned off* so as not to be visible to users. This is the Feature Toggle[4] pattern.

10.1 Simple Feature Toggles

We can implement the most basic form of feature toggles by showing or hiding the entry point to a feature in the UI, using a simple conditional in a template.

```
<c:if test="${featureFoo}">
    <a href="/foo">Foo</a>
</c:if>
```

We can do something similar for simple changes to application logic.

```
public void doSomething() {
    if (featureFoo) {
        «foo specific logic»
    }
    «regular logic»
}
```

For more complicated changes, this approach would likely lead to a hair ball of conditionals infecting every area of the code base. Furthermore, if these conditions persist in the code base long after the features have been delivered or are being kept around *just in case*, eventually the entire application will be buried in nested conditionals, leading to code that is impossible to maintain or reason about.

10.2 Maintainable Feature Toggles

For more extensive changes, we should use inheritance or composition to extend the existing code with feature-specific functionality, refactoring where necessary to provide clean extension points.

We could add an extension point that we can leverage via inheritance.

```
public interface Processor {
    void process(Bar bar);
}
```

---

3. http://jawspeak.com/tag/trunk-based-development/
4. http://martinfowler.com/bliki/FeatureToggle.html

```
public class CoreProcessor implements Processor {
    public void process(Bar bar) {
        doSomething(bar);
        handleFoo(bar);
        doSomethingElse(bar);
    }

    protected void handleFoo(Bar bar) {
    }
}

public class FooProcessor extends CoreProcessor {
    protected void handleFoo(Bar bar) {
        doSomethingFooSpecific(bar);
    }
}
```

Or we could use composition to achieve the same thing.

```
public interface FeatureHandler {
    void handle(Bar bar);
}

public class Processor {
    FeatureHandler handler;

    public Processor(FeatureHandler handler) {
        this.handler = handler;
    }

    public void process(Bar bar) {
        doSomething();
        handler.handle(bar);
        doSomethingElse();
    }
}

public class CoreHandler implements Handler {
    public void handle(Bar bar) {
    }
}

public class FooHandler implements Handler {
    public void handle(Bar bar) {
        doSomethingCompletelyDifferent(bar);
    }
}
```

Dependency Injection

We can now leverage our Dependency Injection[5] container to do most of the feature-specific configuration for us. Let's take a look at how we might be able to do this in Spring MVC.

One option is to add separate applicationContext-${feature}.xml files for feature-specific bean definitions. In some situations, however, we will be dealing with lists of beans, such as the list of interceptors. Duplicating this list in a feature-specific context file will create maintenance problems.

You're better off leaving the list in the base applicationContext.xml file. When a feature needs to add an interceptor, we can add it to the main list, define the bean in the feature-specific context file, and define a *null implementation*[6] in the core context file.

Annotations

We can also leverage annotations and eliminate the need to repeat ourselves in XML by creating marker annotations for our features. We will use the value of the annotation to indicate whether we want the annotated component when the feature is turned on or off.

FeatureTogglesInPractice/annotation/Foo.java
```
@Retention(RetentionPolicy.RUNTIME)
public @interface Foo {
    boolean value() default true;
}
```

We also need to create a custom TypeFilter that will use the feature toggle information and our annotation to include the correct implementation...

FeatureTogglesInPractice/annotation/FeatureIncludeFilter.java
```
public class FeatureIncludeFilter implements TypeFilter {

    private final TypeFilter fooFilter = new AnnotationTypeFilter(Foo.class, true);

    public boolean match(MetadataReader metadataReader,
                         MetadataReaderFactory metadataReaderFactory)
        throws IOException {

        if (fooFilter.match(metadataReader, metadataReaderFactory)) {
            boolean value = getAnnotationValue(metadataReader, Foo.class);

            if (FeatureToggles.isFooEnabled()) {
                return value;
```

---

5.   http://martinfowler.com/articles/injection.html
6.   http://en.wikipedia.org/wiki/Null_Object_pattern

```
        } else {
            return !value;
        }
    }
    return false;
}

private boolean getAnnotationValue(MetadataReader metadataReader,
                            Class annotationClass) {
    return (Boolean) metadataReader.
        getAnnotationMetadata().
        getAnnotationAttributes(annotationClass.getName()).
        get("value");
    }
}
```

and add our type filter to the spring component scanner configuration.

```
<context:component-scan base-package="com.example.features">
  <context:include-filter type="custom"
                        expression="com.example.features.FeatureIncludeFilter" />
</context:component-scan>
```

Now we can go ahead and annotate our implementations accordingly, and Spring will take care of the rest.

```
public interface Processor {
    «»
}

@Foo(false)
public class CoreProcessor implements Processor {
    «»
}

@Foo
public class FooProcessor extends CoreProcessor {
    «»
}
```

Things can get more interesting when we start adding more features to the mix. We might need to extend the type filter to handle more complex combinations of features.

10.3 Separating Static Assets

In the previous section, we looked at a few approaches for dealing with feature toggles on the server side. But what about static assets like JavaScript and CSS?

We could turn some of the static assets into templates that render server side. This way, we can add logic to modify them in a feature-specific way. But this approach moves static assets that could be hosted on a CDN[7] back to the application server, which might not be acceptable in some scenarios.

We could also turn our static assets into templates that get rendered at build time. This might also be problematic because it locks us in to only being able to toggle features by redeploying.

A better approach is to leave static assets as static files and create feature-specific versions of the static content that we can include conditionally from our dynamic templates. So, we might take shopping_cart.css and create a shopping_cart_foo.css file to provide specific styling for the shopping cart with feature *Foo* enabled.

In the case of JavaScript, we also have the option to use feature conditionals inside JavaScript functions like we do with server-side code. This approach, however, has one major drawback. It leaks information about features that we have in development but are not yet ready to release to end users. Sometimes accidental disclosure is not a big deal, but there are situations where leaking unreleased features early could be catastrophic. Let's take a look at how we can prevent accidental disclosure of unreleased features.

10.4 Preventing Accidental Disclosure

When it comes to secrecy, working in an isolated branch has a natural advantage. It pretty much guarantees that the code developed on a branch will remain secret until the branch is merged back to the main line. Overcoming the fear of accidentally leaking unreleased features is one of the big barriers to replacing feature branches with feature toggles.

The obvious way that unreleased features can leak is by not being properly wrapped in feature toggles. If we are lucky, this will manifest itself as some kind of obvious error. But often the difference will be subtle: some message will contain the wrong text, an extra field will be displayed, and so on.

With extensive manual testing, we will eventually notice the inconsistency. We can also attempt to use automated functional tests, but testing for the absence of functionality or UI elements is tricky.

The really subtle way that unreleased features can leak is through potentially invisible artifacts, such as unused CSS classes, JavaScript code, and even HTML comments. This kind of accidental disclosure can be very hard to notice.

---

7.   http://en.wikipedia.org/wiki/Content_delivery_network

The best way to prevent accidental disclosure is through a disciplined development process. Any work that is done as part of a feature should be wrapped in feature toggles. Modifications to static assets should be done in separate feature-specific files, and the usage of these new files should be wrapped in feature toggles. If we always separate feature-specific static files, we have the option to not even include those files with our deployment, just to be safe.

10.5 Runtime Toggles

Being able to toggle features on and off at runtime allows us to test various features against a single deployed application, either manually or in an automated functional suite. This also allows us to quickly turn off features if something goes wrong in production.

The first question we need to consider about runtime toggling of features is whether users with in-progress sessions will see toggled features immediately or whether feature toggle settings persist for the duration of a session.

Persisting feature toggles for the duration of the session allows the user to see a consistent experience of the website. Toggling features immediately has the downside of possibly confusing users when the website behavior changes out from underneath them. This might also result in application errors because of broken expectations. Toggling features immediately does, however, allow us to quickly turn off a feature globally if something is misbehaving.

A flexible feature toggle system might allow toggles to be applied either immediately or at the end of the session, depending on the urgency of toggling the feature.

We also have to consider how to propagate feature toggles across multiple application servers. We could put feature toggles in a centralized external system like a database or in files that are rescanned periodically.

We could also expose a management interface, such as JMX,[8] where toggles can be changed directly against the running application server. This has the benefit of being able to make changes immediately, but it does require extra coordination to make sure changes are made consistently across an entire fleet of servers. If we are going to toggle features directly against a running application server, we also need to consider persisting feature toggles across application restarts.

---

8. http://en.wikipedia.org/wiki/Java_Management_Extensions

Build-Time Toggles

It is also possible to toggle features at build time. In addition to providing an advantage when it comes to being paranoid about what code gets compiled into the release, build-time toggles are also used when a feature changes the version of a dependency to something that is not API compatible.

10.6 Incompatible Dependencies

Upgrading dependencies to new versions that are not fully backward compatible can be painful, depending on how extensive the changes are. With feature toggles, this problem is amplified because we might find ourselves simultaneously needing to use both versions of a dependency. So, just how to do we go about using two versions of a class that might have different constructors, different method signatures, or different methods altogether?

We could fall back to using reflection for these situations so we can dynamically invoke the correct version and still be able to compile by cheating the static type checker. This, however, introduces both complexity and a performance penalty.

Instead, we can create a wrapper around the classes that have differences. We can start by creating a common interface that exposes everything needed for both features and then create feature-specific implementations that delegate to the appropriate version of our dependency. Then we can separate the feature-specific implementations into separate code modules and at build-time compile only one or the other. This is where build-time toggles are not only useful but necessary.

10.7 Testing of Feature Toggles

One of the common concerns around feature toggles is the potential explosion of combinations that need to be tested. It is true that in theory the number of combinations grows exponentially with the number of features. But in practice this is rarely the case. It only makes sense to test combinations that we expect will actually go live.

It turns out the actual number of combinations we need to test is the same as if we had feature branches. It is just much easier to test because we can do so from a single code base. If we are using runtime toggles, we can even get away with a single build and change features as needed by the various tests.

If we are using build-time toggles, we can create separate build pipelines for each combination, with different smoke and regression suites for each pipeline.

Each commit will trigger a build of all the pipelines. The end result, from a CI point of view, ends up looking the same as if we had to build separate branches.

Unlike separate branches, however, with this setup we have the opportunity for a commit for Feature A to break a test or the build for Feature B. To be fair, this is still a concern with separate branches. But in the case of separate branches, we delay this problem until integration. Feature toggles expose this problem with every commit, which I would argue is a benefit.

10.8 Removing Toggles for Completed Features

Another large barrier to adopting feature toggles is the concern that over time the code will become littered with obsolete toggles. Therefore, it is important to remove toggles that are no longer necessary. After a feature is complete and deployed to production, we might still want to keep the toggle around for a couple of days or weeks, until we are certain that the feature is behaving correctly. After this point, however, we can go ahead and remove the toggles for this feature, collapsing the code into the core version of the application.

To make it easier to rip out obsolete toggles, we can make toggles statically typed. This means having a FeatureToggles.isFooEnabled() method instead of Feature-Toggles.isFeatureEnabled("foo"). This will allow us to leverage the compiler to easily remove obsolete features from code, because as soon as we remove the isFooEnabled() method, any code that still uses it will fail to compile.

We can also leverage our IDE to find usages of the given method in order to find places where this might also need to be removed from templates, if our IDE supports it.

If a feature under development is placed on hold, either indefinitely or for a long period of time, it might be tempting to leave the current state of the feature in the code, guarded by toggles. I believe this is generally a bad idea. Since the code is hiding behind toggles that will not be used for a while, it will easily rot and cause maintenance problem. Instead, we should rip out the code and its corresponding toggles. The old version will always be available in version control for reference.

10.9 Wrapping Up

Sometimes tool features (such as branching in version control) encourage us to use them in ways that harm other engineering practices. Allowing developers to code in isolation on branches leads to problems with integration and merging. Feature toggles allow you to reap the benefits of delaying decisions on features without harming the engineering best practice of continually integrating code.

Feature toggles aren't an excuse to featurize your application to death. When you have decided to include a particular feature, remove the toggles and keep your code clean.

CHAPTER 11

Driving Innovation into Delivery

by Marc McNeill

Innovation: "The act of introducing something new." So reads the dictionary definition. Google returns almost 92 million pages on the term. Innovation is a hot topic.

But how many organizations deliver it? Many large enterprises, even some of the most forward-thinking, suffer *innovation disconnect*, which is when the business innovation being pursued by business leaders fails to deliver on its initial promise.

Return to that dictionary definition of innovation, "the act of introducing something *new*." The enterprise landscape is littered with organizations that can barely *deliver* anything, let alone introduce something new. You don't have to look hard or far to find examples: the retail bank that has spent the past four years working on a replacement for its online banking product and has yet to deliver, the media organization that spent a year designing concepts for its new website before a line of code was written, and so on.

Now go back in time twelve years. Go to Google[1] and see how it describes itself.

"Google Inc. was founded in 1998 by Sergey Brin and Larry Page to make it easier to find high-quality information on the web."

There's nothing there about browsers or phone operating systems or word processors or spreadsheets. It took twelve years to go from a search engine to the Google we know today.

---

1.   Use the Wayback Machine to do this: http://www.archive.org/.

Place that lens over the bank. Have they managed to adapt to the changing world? It's taken four years to introduce something (that's a third of Google's life and almost all Facebook's life) that hasn't even started delivering value. Yet if you talk to the people in the business, they haven't been idle. Customer research, customer insight, visual design, business case development: all these activities take time.

The first *The ThoughtWorks Anthology [Inc08]* kicked off with an essay by Michael Robinson and Roy Singham on "solving the business software last mile," which is the challenges of the path to production, from code complete to live. This essay talks about the other end of the product life cycle: solving the problem of getting innovation into IT and of driving agility into business innovation and business innovation into the delivery process.

11.1 Value Stream or Value Trickle

With the premise that innovation in an enterprise is only as valuable as the ability to deliver it, let's start by looking at how new ideas get delivered today. This means looking to the time before the idea becomes a project for delivery by IT. How does it become a project in the first place? What is the value chain from concept to cash?

As organizations grow, they tend to build departmental silos, for example a marketing function, a product function, channel functions, and so on. Each department of division becomes focused upon their own discrete functions rather than overarching outcomes. Each department commissions their own activities, with outputs presented as deliverables.

Success is the timely production of these deliverables, regardless of the value they add to the actual production of the application. So, for example, in developing a web application, the following may occur:

1. The business starts working on the product idea. Time elapses as it undertakes research, market sizing, and concept development.

2. The business then engages a creative agency. The agency delivers its designs on foam-backed boards that look good in the boardroom at their final presentation. That is often the end of their engagement.

3. A benefits case is produced by the business team (it may be called a business case, but it is rare for IT to be fully engaged at this stage to provide a meaningful estimate and cost for the product).

4. The business produces ever more documentation: project initiation (PID), high-level requirements, solution blueprint, and a bid document to gain

funding (with the further complication of finance allocating funding for projects only at the beginning of the financial year, resulting in additional barriers to getting innovation realized).

Each step of this process, and each document produced, has taken time to produce, with multiple stakeholders engaged. The clock is ticking, and the competition is releasing new innovations to the market. We still have to go through high-level design, detailed design, and so on. *We are several months into the process, and the project is on track. Yet not a line of code has been written.*

Your Value Stream

How do you go about convincing stakeholders that there are indeed inefficiencies in the process and that maybe there is a different, better way of doing things? A first step is getting stakeholders together in a workshop to identify for themselves issues with their current process. This is not a talking shop; it is them walking through the value stream of a project (who did what, how long did it take, and what value was delivered for each activity).

Select a recent project that started with a new business idea and was delivered by IT into production. Get as many of the stakeholders involved in the project (the people who were involved, not who managed it) and walk through all the activities that were undertaken. Give each activity a sticky note. Stick them on a white board and connect them with lines. For each activity, identify who did what, how long each activity took, and what the gap was between activities and hand-offs. Pretty soon you'll start to get a picture of how much time was spent on value-added tasks (that is, getting stuff done that had a material impact on the project) and how much time was spent on waiting and waste (that is, getting multiple people to sign off on a deliverable that was not on the critical path). This is a crude interpretation of *value stream mapping*. It is a simple tool for helping clearly identify how and why enterprise innovation is currently inefficient and lacking creativity and may provide a direction for doing something different.

11.2 A New Approach

So, we have a problem with getting innovation out of the business and research and development and into IT. The problem is that when it gets to IT, the requirements are thrown over the fence from the business with instructions to "build this." We've seen that by applying value stream thinking to this process, there are clear and distinct hand-offs between specialized departments (business analysis, systems analysis, security, etc.) that lead to inefficiency and waste. Too much time, effort, and resources are spent on developing ideas in the business idea factory before they reach the development and delivery engine.

That's easily said, but what's to be done about it? Here are four tips to *delivering* innovation:

- Nurture a culture of collaboration and creative thinking throughout the whole product development life cycle.

- Bring agility (and IT) into product research and discovery, leading to the harvesting of insights and inspiration and developing new concepts and ideas.

- Initiate a rapid project inception to share the vision and identify the minimum requirements to deliver to customers as quickly as possible.

- Develop a virtuous cycle of continuous design, continuous development.

Collaboration Culture

By using lean, agile, and design thinking, we can drive business innovation, which is the ideas factory, closer to IT, which is the delivery engine. Rather than moving innovation through departmental silos, we take a new, rapid, and continuous approach. This means bringing together IT and business representatives right from the start.

Here's something to try. Hand a colleague a sheet of paper and ask her to tear it in half behind her back. You tear a sheet of paper in half behind your back. The same requirement for both of you. Now do the "reveal." I'll put money on it that they have torn their paper across the horizontal plane. Now you show them your tear: you've torn it down the vertical plane. The same requirement, two different interpretations. Words are slippery things, open to interpretation, and yet this is how we work. We come out of meetings thinking we are all agreed.

Collaboration means bringing together a core team right from the start of the product innovation process. This is a social activity. This will probably include a developer, BA, PM, UX, creative/visual designer, and business team consisting of a product owner (a single, empowered individual who will act as "the truth" and the ultimate decision maker for the project) and subject-matter experts dedicated to the project as required. They are together from the product research and idea generation and inception to the product delivery and beyond.

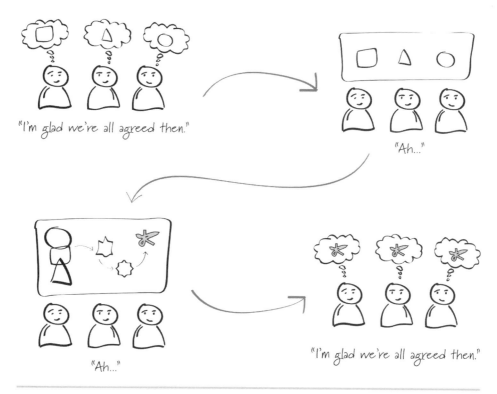

Figure 11—Use visual models to get ideas out of our heads and share the thinking.

Our experience suggests that, for a project of sensible scope, two to four weeks for research and inception of a project is reasonable. Each week starts with a kick-off meeting where we plan the week ahead and concludes with a showcase where we demonstrate to stakeholders the progress made. Each day typically has a series of workshops with either the full stakeholder group or small group analysis on more detailed questions. We follow Agile practices such as stand-ups and showcases. A dedicated project room for the duration is essential; as the days progress, the walls become the workspace, covered with sketches, sticky notes, and artifacts generated through the process. During the discovery, the team produces assumptions that they look to validate through insights. They may test these assumptions by getting out of the building to observe users at work or interview customers as they shop. They might look at analytics on the current process. They may capture insights in the morning and then come back in the afternoon to report to the team. The team documents their findings on sticky notes that can be grouped. They identify common themes and construct further hypotheses to test through the process. This visual approach enables the team to rapidly converge on "what" before moving on to the "how."

As they move from the conceptual to the tangible, they develop visual models of the requirements such as storyboards, sketches, and wireframes (Figure 11, *Use visual models to get ideas out of our heads and share the thinking*, on page 183). These enable the team to gain a joint understanding of the requirements through a visualization of what their vision is. This use of visual modeling techniques is highly effective in allowing diverse stakeholder groups to "speak the same language" and ensure shared understanding.

Agile Product Research and Discovery

Imagine...

Imagine it is 2007, there is no Apple, and you are a new entrant developing a product that will go head to head with Nokia's flagship phone, the N95. You are the product manager who is responsible for the success of the product. You are focused on beating Nokia; you've made it your business to intimately know the N95, and you can recite the list of features it has from memory. You have a meeting with your design team, and they break the news. They tell you the spec they have come up with.

> **You:** Let me get this straight. You are telling me that the phone you are proposing we take to market will have no card slot, no 3G, no Bluetooth, no decent camera, no MMS, no video, no cut and paste, no secondary video camera, no radio, no GPS, no Java...?

> **Team:** Yup. We've ignored feature parity; we've built something that people will actually want to use.

The first generation of iPhone was released in June 2007, three months after Nokia's flagship handset, the N95. On paper, when you compare the phone features side by side, it is a sorry-looking list. As a product manager, would you rather have the iPhone or the N95 on your resume?

Thomas Edison said, "I find out what the world needs. Then, I go ahead and invent it." Where do you find out what the world, *your customers*, need? How do you know what they really want? We may be able to bring innovation to market quickly, but how do we know it is the right? This is where discovery comes in—doing just enough together to understand what is really needed. What follows are some ideas for discovery.

Customer Insight

Like an anthropologist, you can study the behaviors of your application's users to understand what they really need. Here are some techniques to assist your discovery process.

Customers in the Wild

Get out of the office and observe people *in the wild*. Don't just leave this to the UX dude on the project; get everyone out observing. What can you learn from offline interactions that you can apply to online interactions? For example, if you have a retail channel, how do customers go about making purchases? What questions do they ask sales assistants; how is the process different between the "I know what I want" customer and the "I've not a clue, help me decide" customer? Witnessing people interacting with technology can be a sobering experience, especially when you are close to a solution and see someone using it for the first time and struggling with what you consider the basics.

Get into the call center and listen to customer calls. What are customers asking for when they call up?

"Computer Says No"

So, there was this cable telco that bundled TV packages with fancy names. When customers called the call center, they'd say "Hi, I want to add films" or "I want to add sports" and the call center operator couldn't say, "Yes, of course, I'll do it right away." They'd have to translate that into a specific product and work out which bundle they'd need to move to. The system was designed according to the business view of the world rather than the reality of human, customer behavior. (Would they need so much investment in customer services if they'd built decent, delightful products in the first place?)

What Your Colleagues Actually Do

Customers are not the only people we develop products for. What about internal users? A central function may set out corporate processes, but what actually goes on in the workforce? Let's take a trip to a large U.K. supermarket and look at their stock control system.

Million-Dollar Price Markdown

At the end of the day the staff marks down prices on the short-life items (sandwiches, and so on). They have a handheld scanner with a belt printer. Scan item, print label, stick label on item. Well, that's what the process is supposed to be; only this takes time (twenty seconds per item), and when you have a whole shelf to do, it is a chore (twelve items takes four minutes). It's far easier to just write down the new price on a "discount label" with a Sharpie and stick it over the barcode (do the whole shelf in less than a minute).

Where's the problem in that? In fact, three minutes of waste (waiting time) has been eliminated. But it is a problem.

The customer takes the item to checkout, and the markdown label is covering the barcode. The checkout colleague tries to peel it off to scan, but it doesn't peel cleanly. So, she manually enters the SKU and the markdown price. This has taken two minutes for one item, and the queue has grown. Because of the "one in front" policy, they have to open a new checkout, and suddenly that small problem at one end of the value chain is replaced by a bigger, costlier one at the front end.

(Had you not observed this, you would never know that bulk-price markdowns on the handheld device is not a "nice to have." It is a million-dollar requirement.)

Your Customer Hates You

<BankName> makes it darn near impossible to get phone numbers of local branch to make appointment. Customer Service #Fail.

That's a random tweet for a search with the term *Customer service* and the hash tag *fail*. You don't need to have a social media strategy to listen to your customers chattering and telling you how you could improve.

Developing Empathy

It is not always possible to leave the building to observe people interacting with your product or brand. (If you are an online brand, you can hardly hang around in your offline competitors' stores and watch their customers buying.) Instead, you can try to develop customer/user empathy to inform your thinking. Get the team to undertake different tasks to get under the skin of what customers go through. These exercises are as much about the emotional feeling of the customer experience as the product or service interaction.

- For an online shop selling mobile phones, visit phone shops in the shopping mall and tell the rep "Hello, I want a mobile phone." Suspend all your knowledge about phones and tariffs. How do they sell?

- For a travel product, go into a travel agent's and ask for a holiday "somewhere hot and cheap in February." How does the sales assistant guide you through the process of choosing flights, hotels, cross selling insurance, and so on?

- For a bank offering consumer loans, ask to borrow money from someone you don't know. (How does it feel?) Go into a car sales room and look to buy a car on credit. What does it feel like to need a loan?

- For a supermarket, get behind the register for a day. (In the United Kingdom, senior executives in the major supermarkets spend time in the stores over the Christmas period.) What does processing real shopping carts feel like? What do customers ask at checkout?

Creating Personas

With an understanding and empathy for your customers, you can develop personas. These are *pen portraits*, a written description of someone that focuses on their personality traits rather than physical appearance, of customers or users of the system you are going to build. These personas will enable you to root ideas and solutions in the context of their usage.

- For each persona type, what key needs will the product address? How will the needs be satisfied? Is that sufficient for the customer, or do we need to add an extra dimension of product desirability?

- What is the trigger that will make them use the product (and the feature), in other words, to move from being aware of it to using it? And then continue using it on a recurring basis?

- What is the environment it will be used in? For example, consuming content in the living room on a TV (a *lean-back* experience) is different from consuming content on a mobile device on a packed train in the morning (a *lean-forward* experience).

Technical Insights

Customer insights are interesting, but how can you use them to develop a viable and desirable product? Here is the value of IT representation in the process. Based upon the emerging product vision, the developers undertake their own research on the current technical landscape and appropriate technologies that may address these requirements. It is important at this stage not to be overly constrained by the current architecture (this is one reason why businesspeople often object to having IT in creative sessions, because they perceive that IT hinders creativity with their negative "our system can't do that" approach). Good IT representation will allow the business to explore creative ideas, think of potential solutions, and possibly spike them out, killing ideas that are truly not feasible (this is done transparently: IT intimately knows the requirement, and the business hears first hand why it will not proceed).

Competitor Insights

Successful innovation doesn't always mean getting to market first. Nor does it mean reinventing the wheel. Let others do the trail blazing, and you follow fast. Look to leaders in both your own sector and other sectors to see what works and what doesn't. Perform usability testing of competitor products to validate your thinking. There are plenty of examples of what good implementation of common functionality looks like (for example, registration, shopping carts, and login) and plenty of design patterns to take inspiration from.

Looking Within

Enough of customers and inspiration from the outside. Inspiration for innovation can often be found within the organization.

Code Jammin'

Devs Know Best

The CIO of a global investment bank was amazed. In our conversation, he told us, "Twenty percent of my developers are working on open source projects." He was intrigued to discover that many of those projects started from ideas his developers had at the bank. Yet the bank didn't give them the opportunity to develop those ideas, and their open source policies actively dissuaded them from being used in the bank. To get the itch scratched, the developers open sourced the ideas to the outside where they could actually get stuff done.

What if the developer talent could be channeled into the product ideation and development process?

The answer for the CIO was to set up internal code jams, bringing together developers for a couple of days and giving them a choice of business problems and free reign to develop innovative solutions.

Documentation Done

Someone Else's Document Isn't Our Deliverable

The ThoughtWorks consultant met with the client user experience team that was developing personas for a new project. The previous day the consultant had met with the client marketing team that shared with him some of their assets. They had already developed personas that would be appropriate for the project. He was puzzled. "Why not use the personas that have been developed by marketing?" he asked the UX team. "Because they are marketing's personas, not ours," he was told.

This is an extreme story, but it points to the way organizations are happy to duplicate effort in producing documentation and artifacts. Just because the innovation is new does not mean you need to commission new research to reach conclusions that you could probably draw from existing documentation from other parts of the organization that have been conducted in the past. From the outset of any innovation activities, you should be asking what has been done before and asking the team to reach out to their connections within the organization to seek answers.

Developing the Business Case

Organizations spend a lot of time and effort developing the business case for a project. Often the balance is tilted toward the benefits case, with the project costs being projected by a senior architect several promotions removed from the people who will actually develop the solution.

The Business Model Canvas[2] is a useful tool for building the business case out in the open. It presents nine blocks of a business model that can be built

---

2. It can be downloaded from here: http://www.businessmodelgeneration.com/downloads.php.

up on the wall using sticky notes, with the model emerging throughout the discovery and inception process.

Inception

The previous section introduced collaborative activities for rapidly gathering insights and background. The next step is to turn these into a vision, plan, and product. Again, speed is of the essence. The goal is to do just enough to give the team direction to start working on the solution.

Creative Thinking

Tim Brown from IDEO gave the audience at his TED Talk[3] a simple exercise. He asked them to draw a picture of the person sitting next to them. He gave them a minute to do so. He then asked them to show their pictures. "Sorry" was the stock disclaimer as the sketches were revealed. Everyone had an inhibition in showing their work. When it comes to creativity, as we move beyond childhood, we take on board inhibitions and feel more uncomfortable sharing our creative efforts unless we perceive them to be ready or any good. We fear what others will think if our "deliverable" is not ready, is not finished, or is not polished. We fear setting expectations, we fear disappointing, and we build up a chain of sign-off that ends with the HiPPO (the *highest paid person's opinion*) setting direction.

I believe the inception process challenges this thinking. It is based on collaboration, creativity, games, and play. We use games such as those described in *Innovation Games [Hoh06]* and *Gamestorming [Gra10]*, particularly for shaping the project objectives and risk.

For example, to drive out the most important features or product attributes, we may use Product in a Box. Give the team a cereal box covered in white paper and ask them to imagine the product will be sold in this box. Imagine the box is on a supermarket shelf; how would you make it stand out? What does it need to tell customers about the product to sell it? In pairs, the teams design the box and then pitch their boxes to the collected group.

For risk and success criteria, imagine the product is a hot-air balloon. What is the fuel that will make it rise, and what are the ropes that will hold it back? The team put sticky notes on the wall to indicate project risks (the ropes that will hold them back) and the fuel (the success criteria for the project).

---

3. http://www.ted.com/talks/tim_brown_on_creativity_and_play.html

Co-design

We've spent time with customers; we have an understanding of *who*. Now the focus turns to the *do*. We identify and walk through high-value, end-to-end scenarios for each main piece of functionality. Collaboratively, the business and the designers and the developers rapidly sketch out ideas on white boards or paper to stimulate thinking: what would we expect the user to do next? This may start as simple boxes and arrows to illustrate flows before moving on to wireframe sketches of potential screens (more often than not, the software that is being developed is manifested as a user interface, so it makes sense to use that as a basis for driving out requirements).[4] Indeed, these sketches can be presented to people outside the immediate group to test the thinking. Do others *get* the concepts we are trying to develop; is the functionality we are considering usable?

The team uses insights and sketches to evolve the product vision. As it becomes more clearly articulated, it is decomposed into stories that describe the requirements. With the collaborative nature of the process, the whole team is involved in the emergent design and capturing of requirements. This process removes ambiguity and uncertainty in what is required and what the stories actually mean. More importantly, the developers understand the context and the intent behind the stories because they are there—and can input into the process, suggesting how technology can enhance the experience. (Often businesspeople will articulate their requirements based on what they know of existing technical implementations rather than technical innovations that can enhance experiences.) In addition to the functional requirements, the whole team participates in a session to draw out nonfunctional requirements. Where appropriate, developers perform technical spikes to validate architecture and design approaches prior to estimation and planning.

Story Estimation

As the team identifies stories, the technical members provide feasibility, high-level design, and estimates for each story. Because they have been involved in the workshops and participated in the business requirements being discussed, they are in a better position to provide estimates for the stories. The developers relatively size the stories (capturing assumptions to support their thinking in the process). Once they have relative estimates, they estimate the team's potential velocity. For a given team size, how many stories do they think they could complete in an iteration? They play this game multiple times

---

4.   Jason Furnell, a fellow ThoughtWorker, shows the process of co-design in a time-lapsed video on his blog at http://tinyurl.com/co-design-workshop.

to arrive at an average velocity. With velocity and estimated stories, the team has the tools to plan a release. Inevitably, the number of stories they have captured far exceeds the time scales (or budget) they wanted to work against, and besides, they need to agree on what they should work on first. It is time to prioritize.

Prioritization

Based upon the estimates, we work as a team to prioritize the requirements that will deliver the highest business value while grouping them into meaningful chunks of functionality that would deliver a compelling customer experience or useful business functionality. Bad experiences with IT often lead the business to believe that anything given a low priority is effectively being descoped, and thus the business is reluctant to mark anything low. The "buying features" in *The Innovation Game [Hoh06]* can help the team understand the cost associated with the requirements they want. We lay out the estimated story cards on the table, collected into themes that meet a user goal (remember that individual stories picked from a backlog do not make a compelling product). Each card has a price (the estimate) attached. We then give the product owner real coins to the value of an initial notional release, and she buys the requirements she desires with the coins she's been given.

Minimal Viable, Desirable Product

The only real value in any innovation is getting it to market. Agreeing on the minimum viable desirable product to take to market is difficult. Often it is not clear why we are doing the prioritization. The business wants the project with all its features; otherwise, why would it have identified them in the first place? To be successful, the minimum viable product should constitute a meaningful, coherent, and desirable collection of requirements that drive business benefit. The process of prioritization may be easy; convincing the product owner that it is possible to release functionality incrementally is often a harder sell. Arguments against this approach include the following:

We can't afford negative reaction. This is particularly heard when launching a mobile application into an app store. There is a fear that if you launch a product that attracts significant negative feedback when it is first launched, it is effectively a dead product from the start. This is a valid concern; however, when you review product feedback that consumers give, it usually centers around the experience they have with the product shipped, such as issues with what it *does*, rather than what it *does not*. People complain that products aren't usable, are buggy, and are hard to use. They don't complain that they don't have features. Getting the basic product right and introducing new feature *enhancements* later is preferable to releasing a fully featured product that fails to delight.

We can't deliver a half-baked solution. This is a legitimate concern that can be addressed by your release strategy. You will have passionate advocates for your brand. You will have customers who would be delighted to be engaged in helping you develop and test new products. This is a model that start-ups often engage: commence with an initial closed beta. You invite people to participate and provide them with access to the application with the full knowledge that it is beta and still under development. The benefit of this process is that you can gather customer feedback and insights based upon real data early on in the process.

We need to have feature parity. There is often a fear that existing customers will not accept a new product that does not have all the existing functionality; ergo, there is no minimum viable product. Identifying what your most valuable customers want and delivering them a beta can overcome this fear, again taking advantage of their goodwill and desire to be part of getting something better and helping them achieve the most arduous or frequent tasks that they currently undertake. Where the strategy is to introduce an existing product into a user base that has no prior experience with your product, consider this approach: what your new customers don't know, they won't expect. Focusing on the customer goal and providing delight in achieving that goal is of greater value than delivering functionality they won't immediately need. Those enhancements can come later.

Continuous Design, Continuous Delivery

In three to four weeks, we have taken a nascent idea to a researched and tested concept with defined requirements and a plan for implementation. We are now ready to start development following an Agile approach.

Where the product success depends heavily on the success of the user interface, it makes sense to get feedback from the start. By building out static HTML templates, styling, and quick and dirty JavaScript functionality early on, the product can be tested with customers much sooner, enabling many iterations of feedback before the stories are played. (This customer testing does not have to be expensive and time-consuming; you can realize significant benefits in performing guerrilla usability testing—going out to the public, for example in coffee shops, and asking people to try the product.) The HTML and CSS assets can then be shared across the prototype and the development code base. You may question this with the concern that by showing a complete and styled UI before you have developed the stories, we are setting expectations that you may not meet. However, if we have been working collaboratively as a team with all stakeholders, this becomes a nonissue. Furthermore, by doing this, there are far fewer changes at implementation time and often a reduction of scope as users respond negatively to innovative ideas that don't work for customers in the UI during usability testing.

Getting a release out should be seen as little more than a significant milestone, not the end goal. Once we are in production, we strive for a regular heartbeat of delivery. Rather than moving from a project to business as usual, the boundaries between these merge. In production we now have usage data, and feedback from the users changes to what is not working and enhancements to what it does. Gone are the days when an analyst had to specify the precise order of elements on a screen; performing split A/B testing or multivariate testing where different users see different versions of the product enables us to make data-driven decisions about what the optimum layout or functionality is. The practices of doing discovery and co-design for new features continue as required, resulting in a virtuous cycle of continuous design, continuous development, and continuous delivery.

11.3 Wrapping Up

Think big, start small, fail fast, or scale fast.

All too often the business innovation being pursued by business leaders fails to deliver on its initial promise. We can no longer blame this on IT. The Agile software development movement has demonstrated how IT can deliver responsively and rapidly. This essay has tried to show how we can bring together customer-driven innovation and Agile practices. It starts with a vision, which is a picture of what we strive for, and then focuses on getting a minimum viable (and delightful) product to customers as soon as possible. In the hands of customers, we rapidly get feedback and the confidence to either continue with the product or kill it cheaply, before sinking too much cost into it. Ultimately, the only value of any product development process is getting the right product into the hands of customers.

Part IV

Data Visualization

The final entry explores the increasingly important area of data visualization and shows how to create compelling visualizations from technical artifacts.

CHAPTER 12

A Thousand Words

by Farooq Ali

Data is no longer scarce. Insight is. Twitter clocks more than 36,000 tweets a minute. Tesco generates more than 2 million records of transaction data every day. By the time you're done reading this page, YouTubers will have uploaded more than 20 hours of video online. And as more companies integrate their systems or embrace the semantic Web, it's becoming increasingly difficult to make sense of all the information out there.

A lot of what we do at ThoughtWorks is help our customers integrate, simplify, and capitalize on these systems and the massive amounts of data they hold, and we rely on information visualization, or *infovis*. Information visualization will play an increasingly important role in dealing with the dataglut. The potent combination of images, words, and numbers—done right—can provide the most meaningful insight into our data. The question is, how do we determine that magic combination? The common misconception is that this task is best left to the designers or aesthetically inclined on the team. But while creative thinking is required, there needs to be method to the designers' madness, in other words, a structured way of approaching the visualization problem in which form follows function. A team that employs visualizations *and a visualization design process* is well on its way to building more innovative and valuable software.

The goal of this chapter is to help demystify information visualization and share some of the structured thinking that goes into designing visualizations. I hope it motivates you to understand infovis and develop a shared vocabulary with others to discuss and create better visualizations.

12.1 Smelling the Coffee

Much infovis work is driven by scientific and academic research. That's fortunate, because infovis is directly linked to human visual perception, which science has learned a lot about in the past century.

What's unfortunate is that the same can't be said wholeheartedly about the IT industry, because its progress in this space is driven less by the objective research conducted in the field and more by the deals between software vendors and CIOs on golf courses. The IT industry has made real advances in data-centric activities such as collecting, cleaning, transforming, integrating, and storing data, but it still lags behind in the human-centric analysis of that data. The brutal truth is that many of the BI tools out there won't withstand the slightest scrutiny when evaluated from the lens of current research in visual perception, design, and effective visual communication.

To borrow from Daniel Pink's famous quote, there is a big gap between what science knows and what businesses are doing. As a result, many of us have given in to the status quo of tabular applications, pie chart presentations, and paginated data. But not all of us. Stephen Few, a contemporary expert in business infovis, says, "Few situations frustrate me more than good infovis research that could solve real problems but remains unknown and unused because it has never been presented to those who need it or has been presented only in ways that people can't understand."

But there are encouraging signs. Infovis is not a new field. Visually communicating information has been around for as long as humans have been telling stories. And there is a resurgence taking place right now toward leveraging infovis in new and deeper ways to address the plethora of data we're overloaded with in this Information Age. Many industries and organizations already understand the value that infovis brings to the table and are using it to solve challenging problems.

When ThoughtWorks is brought in for assessments of large-scale IT projects facing difficulties, we first use the latest research in internal software quality measurement and infovis to diagnose the current "health" of the system. As you can imagine, information that comes in such a complex form—a spaghetti of architectures, hundreds of thousands of lines of code, and years of human decisions and implementation history—is not easy to analyze. This is why we rely on good infovis practices to excavate the insight that helps top-level decision makers make the right choices.

Similarly, the *New York Times* has earned a reputation for telling insightful stories about the world by revealing patterns and relationships in the light of current events. Today's cutting-edge retail analytics companies, such as those working with loyalty programs, use infovis extensively to help retailers "perfectly" price, promote, and place products in their stores based on consumer-buying habits and loyalty. And now with the widespread adoption of touch-screen media and small-screen ubiquitous interfaces, we're being pushed to find even more innovative ways to visualize information.

So, what are some winning design principles in information visualization?

12.2 Visualization Design Principles

"Evidence is evidence, whether words, numbers, images, diagrams, still or moving," says Edward Tufte, the design and infovis guru. "The information doesn't care what it is, the content doesn't care what it is. It is all information." The goal of information visualization is to help us think more productively and analyze information more efficiently. In discussing the ways to reach these goals, it's worth keeping the following principles in mind:

- *Increase information density*: Not everything in a visualization has a purpose. Charts, especially Microsoft's autogenerated ones, are often littered with what Tufte calls *chart junk*—visual elements that communicate nothing about the information. Another way to think about this principle is in terms of maximizing the data-to-ink ratio, in other words, the ratio of ink (or pixels) that encodes meaningful information about the data vs. the total ink (or pixels) used. Typical bad examples are 3D bar charts, graphs with useless pictorial backgrounds, redundant gridlines, and overused icons. Resist redundant bells and whistles, and be more cognizant of how you use each pixel.

- *Leverage visual thinking*: The human vision system is wired to recognize features and patterns in everything it sees, much of it before you even get to "think" about (*aka* attentively process) the visual information. If we visually represent our information just the right way to exploit our prewired visual processing, we allow the viewer to analyze the information more efficiently and by "thinking" less. This is the quintessence of human-centric analysis and what most of this essay will focus on. We'll see how a structured visualization design process helps maximize visual thinking to make us analyze information more productively.

- *The content is the interface*: Visual thinking addresses the reading, or consumption, of information, but consuming isn't enough. We want to interact with our data. The human-centric approach to this is to create natural and immersive interfaces. When you use Google Maps on the iPhone/iPad, the gestures of pinching, swiping, and tapping the map feel natural. The direct manipulation and immediate feedback from interacting with the map is an example of the content being the interface. While not as effective, this principle is just as important for mouse-controlled displays: think context-sensitive tooltips, linked highlighting, overlays, and animated transitions. The goal of this principle is make the content the focus of attention, to the point that the tool simply "disappears."

12.3 The Visualization Design Process

For the most part, the process of designing visualizations touches on all parts of the software development value stream. At the end of the day, information visualization is simply the process of transforming data into an interactive visual representation, either through code or through a tool. Several people have spent the time to define structured processes for creating visualizations such as the Pipeline Model (Agrawala), Cyclical Model (Wijk), and Nested Model (Munzner). Because some of these processes were initially described in research papers, they can be unnecessarily cryptic (at least for most of us) and give the impression that their authors were trying really hard to impress the reader (one of them even uses calculus!).

Cutting through the cruft of unnecessary complexity, the essence of the visualization design processes is shown in Figure 12, *Visualization design process*, on page 200.

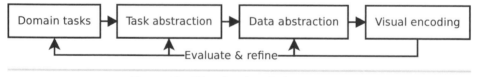

Figure 12—Visualization design process

Define Domain Tasks

A good visualization always starts by articulating a need in the business's natural domain language. Borrowing from the Agile methodology, one way to articulate those needs can be in the form of user stories, such as "As a school teacher, I want to know how well my students are doing in my class so that I can plan the midterm review session accordingly."

Task Abstraction

Obviously, knowing how well students are doing in class can be measured in many ways. I may want to determine the average performance of the class. I may want to know the extent to which those grades vary across students, topics, or over time. I may want to see who has been absent when I taught things that aren't covered in their textbook. I may want to know the topics that students are having most difficulty with. Do you see a similarity between the tasks the teacher is trying to perform and the tasks a project manager, financial analyst, or anybody else performs on a daily basis? Analytical tasks are usually just instances or a mix of a few well-known abstract tasks performed on one or more metrics. Most of those are as follows:

- *Filter*: Find data that satisfies conditions.
- *Find extremum*: Find data with extreme values.
- *Sort*: Rank data according to some metric.
- *Determine range*: Find the span of data values.
- *Find anomalies*: Find outliers and data with unexpected values.
- *Characterize distribution*: Determine how the data is distributed over the spectrum of available information.
- *Cluster*: Group similar items together.
- *Correlate*: Recognize a relationship between two types of information.
- *Scan*: Quickly review a set of items.
- *Set operations*: Find set intersections, unions, and so on.
- *Retrieve value*: Look up a specific value based on some criteria.

The goal of task abstraction is to break down the domain task into a set of low-level abstract tasks/operations, preferably ranked by priority if possible. As we'll see later, visually encoding your data effectively relies heavily on the analytical task(s) being addressed.

Data Abstraction

How many different ways can you give me the temperature of water? Taps give you two: hot and cold. You could also say it's boiling, hot, lukewarm, cold, or frozen. Or you could just call it out in degrees Fahrenheit/Celsius. How would you arrange the words *hot* and *cold* in order? How about boiling, cold, lukewarm, hot, and frozen—which one comes first? Try -1°C, 10°C, and 4°C. The way in which we represent our data has a profound implication on how we cognitively process it, especially when visualized. Before we start to visually encode data, we need to understand the nature of each metric (*aka* data type) in it. There are three essential data types we need to know about.

- *Nominal data*: Categorical data in which the order does not matter, for example, apples vs. oranges; the departments of sales, engineering, marketing, and accounting.

- *Ordinal data*: Data in which the order matters but not the degree of difference between the values. Customer satisfaction that is measured as "very satisfied," "satisfied," "neutral," "unsatisfied," and "very unsatisfied" does not indicate how much more or less satisfied one is than another. Likewise, representing the winners of a race as first, second, and third doesn't indicate the difference in race times associated with the positions.

- *Quantitative data*: Numerical data in which the difference between the values is meaningful, for example 1cm, 10cm, and 20cm. Quantitative data is sometimes further categorized into interval data and ratio data to indicate the existence of an explicit 0 point, but we'll keep it simple here.

Sometimes we get the choice of transforming data types from our data set based on our task abstractions. You might be wondering why or when you would want to do that. The following are two common scenarios:

- A task requires making some assumptions about the data set in order to aggregate information, such as calculating averages and sums. For example, an Agile team might assign quantitative values to T-shirt-sized effort estimates of user stories based on geometric progression (for example, S=1, M=2, L=4, XL=8) in order to quantify the project scope.

- A task does not require precision in order to be performed effectively. For example, the task of determining which employees submitted their timesheets late might not need to know how late the submissions were. This is where design perfection comes in and why it's so important to clearly articulate your tasks. Companies like Apple get this because it shares the following sentiment:

    > "A designer knows he has achieved perfection not when there is nothing left to add, but when there is nothing left to take away."

    —*Antoine de Saint-Exupery*

Understanding your data types and choosing the right level of abstraction (that is, data types) from your data set based on tasks are key ingredients to effectively visualizing data. For example, the following visualizations are two different ways of showing your company's brand power (weak, medium, strong) and revenue by city. Without giving you any extra information about the bar chart on the left (A), can you guess in which city you're generating the most revenue with the weakest brand power?

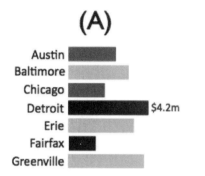 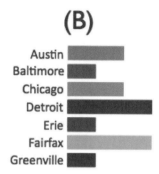

Chances are you guessed Greenville because it has the longest bar among the lightest ones. There are a couple of things at play here. First, humans intuitively associate variations in color intensity (how light or dark something is) with ordinal data (brand power). Plus, our vision system is very good at differentiating color intensity (up to a limit). Similarly, our vision system is tuned to discerning the smallest of differences in lengths of objects, which makes length a great choice for visually representing (*aka* visually encoding) quantitative data types—revenue in this case. If I were to switch the visual encodings around—shown in (B)—and use length for brand power and color intensity for revenue, it would be a lot more difficult, if not impossible, to perform the same task.

In fact, you can try to ask any question for this data, and the first visualization will invariably do a better job at answering it, even if I gave you a detailed legend for the second one. Leveraging our visual powers to rapidly perceive information based on the task and data abstractions allows us to pack more information in less space as well as detect patterns that would otherwise have to be processed by the left side of our brain (the analytical and sequential side). This is precisely what the next step of visual encoding tries to achieve.

Visual Encoding

Simply put, visual encoding is the process of mapping data onto our visual field, usually on 2D surfaces. Effective visual encoding requires some understanding of how vision works in the first place. As with many of the topics in this essay, I can't do justice to the depth of this topic in a few paragraphs. But for the purpose of this essay, here's all we need to understand: visual perception is essentially a three-stage process.

1. Feature extraction
2. Pattern perception
3. Goal-directed processing

In the first stage of feature extraction, millions of neurons work in parallel to detect primitive visual features such as color, form, and motion. This is best explained by a typical example: how many 3s do you see in the following set of numbers?

12904489770478921782372549682584514907601305498
70217144885514907675230876878562468425728189875
41687090010047892178047121536989602439740951287

How long did that take you? There should be five. Now try it again.

12904489770478921782**3**72549682584514907601**3**05498
702171448855149076752**3**0876878562468425728189875
41687090010047892178047121**5**36989602439740951287

Obviously, that was a lot easier, thanks to the first stage of feature extraction during which your vision system did some of the thinking for you, also known as *preattentive processing*. Making something lighter or darker (that is, changing its color intensity) is one way of visually encoding information for preattentive processing, which is why color intensity is also referred to as a *preattentive attribute*. The reason it was more difficult the first time is that the shapes of numbers are complex objects that your brain can't preattentively process. In his book *Information Visualization: Visual Thinking for Design [War08]*, Colin Ware suggests seventeen preattentive attributes. The most relevant ones, narrowed down by Stephen Few in *Information Dashboard Design [Few06]*, are shown in Figure 13, *Preattentive attributes (Stephen Few)*, on page 205.

In the second stage of pattern perception, our brain segments the visual world into distinct regions and discovers the structure of objects and the connections between them. It's only in the third stage that the information is processed by our brain's attentive processes to perform the analytical task at hand.

Our goal is to make the most of the first two stages to let the preattentive processing do some thinking on our behalf and to convey information in big visual gulps so that we can understand our data more efficiently.

Encoding for Feature Extraction

It turns out that the effectiveness of these attributes varies based on the data type you want to encode. So, how do we know which ones to pick for what?

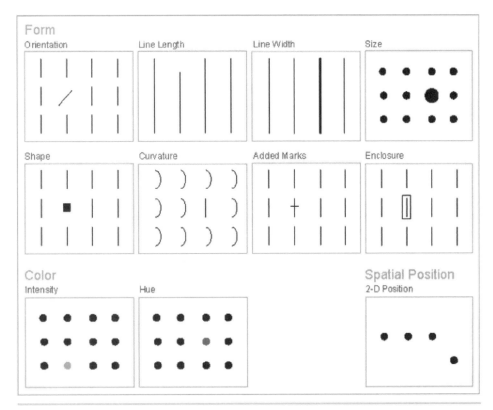

Figure 13—Preattentive attributes (Stephen Few)

I find Mackinlay's rankings (Figure 14, *Mackinlay's rankings (Mackinlay)*, on page 206) easiest to elucidate the concept because the rankings also show how the effectiveness varies by data type.

For novices like myself, this is the holy grail of visualization design. Take a minute to explore the rankings and relate them to your own experience. As you can see, 2D position is at the top of the list for all types. This is why traditional X-Y graphs are so effective at conveying so many kinds of information. Also notice how length and density (previously called *color intensity*) vary for quantitative and ordinal data types, a fact used in the example of brand power and cities given earlier.

Let's use these rankings to evaluate a common myth about the effectiveness of pie charts for quantitative comparisons. Pie charts use area and angle as a means to convey quantitative data. However, based on the rankings, both length and position trump area and angle. Let's see for ourselves: using the

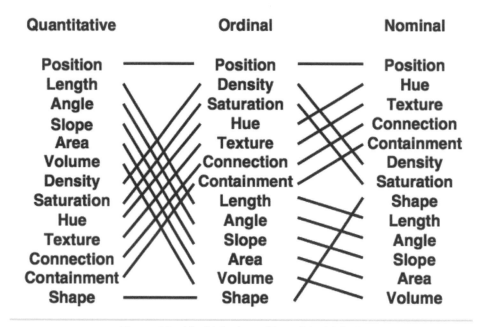

Figure 14—Mackinlay's rankings (Mackinlay)

pie chart in Figure 15, *Find the Software Feature Cost*, on page 207, can you tell which software feature is costing you the most to build?

Probably not. It's clearly easier to answer that question using the bar chart instead. Arguably, pie charts are effective for visualizing part-to-whole relationships, such as the fact that three of the previous features cost approximately 25 percent each, but that's about it. If the task at hand requires more information that's just as important for your tasks, such as comparing or ranking the parts, you should encode your data differently.

Picking the most effective encodings relies heavily on the task at hand, so even the encoding rankings should be seen in that light. Also keep in mind that you can encode a data type with more than one visual channel to help perform the task more efficiently. For example, you could encode a quantitative temperature with length, hue (blue or red), and intensity (diverging from light to dark in both directions—hot and cold).

Encoding for Pattern Recognition

The Gestalt principles of visual perception are very useful for grouping, linking, and distinguishing information in visualizations using our vision system's second stage of pattern recognition. For example, you might want to guide the user toward scanning information horizontally vs. vertically. You could

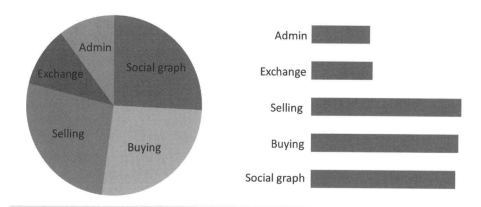

Figure 15—Find the Software Feature Cost

do this simply by allocating slightly more vertical than horizontal spacing to help the viewer group the information preattentively. This phenomenon is explained by the Gestalt principle of proximity, since the objects placed closer to each other are perceived as belonging to the same group. Or you could just group the information with lines or borders using the principle of enclosure. The six Gestalt principles are best explained using visual examples (Figure 16, *Gestalt principles of pattern perception*, on page 207).

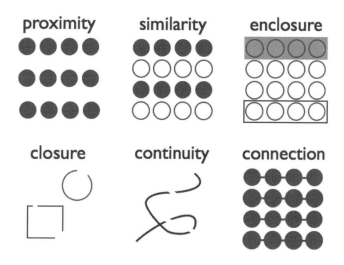

Figure 16—Gestalt principles of pattern perception

- *Proximity*: We see three rows of dots instead of four columns of dots because they are closer horizontally than vertically.

- *Similarity*: We see similar-looking objects as part of the same group.

- *Enclosure*: We group the first four and last four dots as two rows instead of eight dots.

- *Closure*: We automatically close the square and circle instead of seeing three disconnected paths.

- *Continuity*: We see one continuous path instead of three arbitrary ones.

- *Connection*: We group the connected dots as belonging to the same group.

The reason scatter plots are so effective in helping us spot correlation in our information is that the laws of proximity, continuity, and similarity allow us to group and fill in the blanks in our data. A visualization inspired by Hans Rosling's famous TED talk on new insights into poverty is shown in Figure 17, *Gestalt principles used to spot correlations in scatterplots*, on page 208.[1]

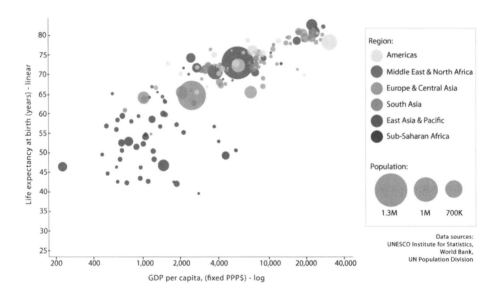

Figure 17—Gestalt principles used to spot correlations in scatterplots

Notice how the arrangement of the dots appears to us naturally as a line. Despite the "noise" from variance, we're still able to visually establish some

1. www.ted.com/talks/hans_rosling_reveals_new_insights_on_poverty.html

correlation between income per person and life expectancy at birth. The correlation is even more evident when the visualization is played as a motion chart, showing change over time. If you haven't already, I highly recommend watching the talk and asking yourself whether you could tell the same story as effectively with just numbers and words.

Evaluate and Refine

As with any good software development process, feedback loops in the process are critical. It's beyond the scope of this essay to delve into the feedback process for software in general. But in infovis, some testing can be conducted fairly objectively with users. Here are some things to keep in mind:

- Incorporate feedback very early and often throughout all stages of development using visual prototypes. Don't underestimate the power of paper sketch testing. Avoid developing "The Perfect Visualization" in the dark only to pull the curtains on something that does not address the domain problem effectively.

- Measuring the time it takes to perform the finer-grained tasks that make up the domain tasks can be useful for testing a set of different encodings for the same information.

- Try creating a battery of test scenarios for different data sets to see how the effectiveness of your encodings in solving the tasks varies.

- Even though we didn't talk about the quality and truthfulness of the data being visualized, remember that data and metrics aren't always right (*a la* "lies, damn lies, and statistics"). As such, they should be taken with a grain of salt; project management and code quality metrics are good examples. Sometimes spotting trends and outliers is more important than tracking absolute numbers, which infovis is great for.

- Understand that there is always an element of subjectivity in user experience because of aesthetic preferences and opinions.

12.4 Visualization Design Patterns

Now that we have a basic understanding of the low-level visualization design process, it's worth taking a look at a small sample of common visualizations for common tasks and get a feel for what's out there. I'm using the phrase *design patterns* loosely here, from the perspective that they provide a reusable visualization skeleton for common tasks and data sets by providing some predefined encodings and then leave the rest up to the designer.

As with any design pattern, I want to caution you that there is no silver bullet. Before using any of these patterns, it is imperative to articulate the tasks and let those tasks guide you. It can be very tempting to slap a beautiful-looking horizon graph for a small data set on your page when all you need is a simple time series chart. Similarly, always ask yourself whether a table can help perform some task (for example, lookups) more effectively.

Exploring Change over Time

Asking our data if something is increasing, decreasing, or remaining stable over time is a very common task. In general, lines do a good job of visually representing time because they adhere to our general perception of time being a continuous entity. Changes through time can be detected by the (preattentively processed) angle of upward and downward slopes that give the data shape.

- *Line graphs*: These encode time and one or more dependent variables with 2D position.

- *Stack graphs (aka finger charts)*: These work like a line graph for multiple metrics, additionally encoding differences in those metrics with area. One example of their effective use is for spotting bottlenecks in a value stream (for example, analysis, development, QA, business signoff in a software development process) by plotting the work completed over time and looking for areas in time that are relatively smaller than their counterparts. A derivative of a stack graph is the steam graph, where the baseline (0 point) is allowed to move freely on the y-axis. The music recommendation service Last.fm uses steam graphs to visualize listening trends.

- *Horizon graphs*: Shown in Figure 18, *Horizon graph (©2012 Panopticon Software AB)*, on page 211, a horizon graph is a better choice for visualizing a large set of time-series data, such as the performance of thirty stocks over a year. It's a form of time-series graph that uses color intensity and area to make us perceive a larger range of y-axis values without stretching the height of the graph. One of the interesting properties of color is that humans tend to overestimate the area of shapes with intense, saturated colors. A horizon graph leverages this phenomena to pack more information in a smaller space, keeping the height of the graph constant. Large quantitative values are encoded with layers of area under a line with varying color. In addition, it mirrors negative values onto the positive axis with a different color (for example, red for negative and blue for positive).

Figure 18—Horizon graph (©2012 Panopticon Software AB)

- *Sparklines*: Shown in Figure 19, *Sparklines used in Google Analytics dashboard*, on page 211, sparklines are intended to be "small, high-resolution graphics embedded in a context of words, numbers, and images," according to Edward Tufte, a well-known expert on visual information design. Sparklines have become very common over the last few years and usually show up in the form of small multiples. They are particularly relevant in dashboards, such as the one provided by Google Analytics for tracking website traffic.

Figure 19—Sparklines used in Google Analytics dashboard

Exploring Correlations

We're not always trying to measure change over time. Sometimes we need to explore the correlation between nominal and ordinal data types. Oftentimes the analysis involves many more conditions and variables too (aka multivariate data). Two commonly used patterns for this are as follows:

- *Scatterplots*: We saw an example of these in Figure 17, *Gestalt principles used to spot correlations in scatterplots*, on page 208. By the same token, scatterplots are great for spotting outliers and anomalies. In its most basic form, a scatterplot uses 2D position to encode quantitative data. However, it provides a lot more encoding options for multivariate data, for example, size/area, shape, color, and enclosure, which is why bubble charts are just a derivative of scatterplots.

- *Matrices*: A matrix works like a scatterplot but divides the 2D space into a grid to accommodate nominal and ordinal data types. Two common forms for exploring correlations are matrix charts and heat matrices. A typical example of a matrix chart is a feature comparison for competing products. A heat matrix (Figure 20, *Heat matrix showing educational performance of Australian students by state/territory*, on page 213), like a heat map (Figure 24, *Heat map showing changes in NASDAQ stocks on a given day*, on page 216), encodes a quantitative or ordinal of interest (represented as a node on the grid) with color. Unlike a heat map, a heat matrix focusses on establishing the correlation between two groups of information, so the 2D position of the node matters, for example showing the profitability of a retail company across product lines (nominal) and regions (nominal).

Exploring Hierarchical and Part-to-Whole Relationships

Thinking in terms of hierarchies and part-to-whole relationships is something we're all good at because the physical world is filled with analogies for our mind to use. Your cell phone's battery doesn't drain like liquid in a container. Your computer's folders of folders and files aren't actually organized neatly that way on your hard drive. But the metaphors make it easy for us to work with the information. Likewise, visualizing information this way is just as helpful, especially for the tasks of clustering, finding anomalies, and set operations. Aside from pie charts, the following are two useful patterns for exploring part-to-whole relationships and hierarchical data:

- *Tree maps*: We can see one example of a tree map in Figure 21, *Tree map*, on page 214. Another interesting use of tree maps is to visualize code

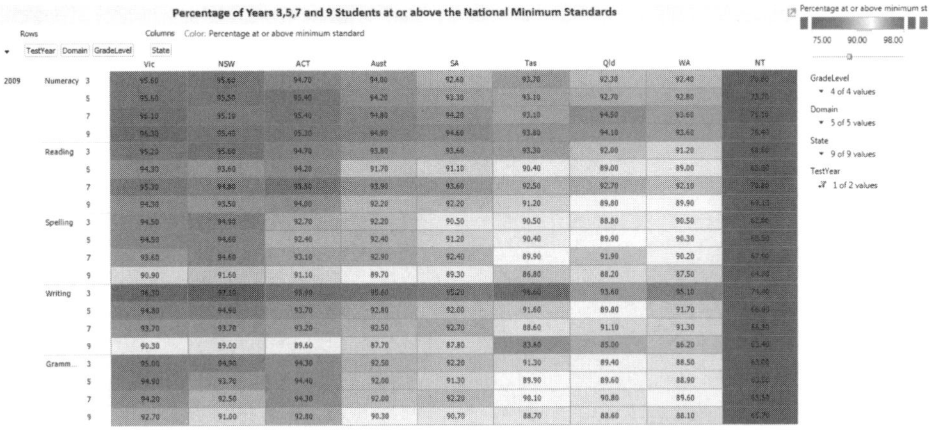

Percentage of Years 3,5,7 and 9 Students at or above the National Minimum Standards

Rows | Columns | Color: Percentage at or above minimum standard

TestYear Domain GradeLevel | State

Percentage at or above minimum st...

75.00   90.00   98.00

			Vic	NSW	ACT	Aust	SA	Tas	Qld	WA	NT
2009	Numeracy	3	95.60	95.90	94.70	94.00	92.60	93.70	92.30	92.40	70.60
		5	95.10	93.50	95.40	94.20	93.30	93.10	92.70	92.80	73.55
		7	96.10	95.10	95.40	94.80	94.20	92.10	94.50	93.60	73.15
		9	96.30	95.45	95.20	94.90	94.60	93.80	94.10	93.60	76.40
	Reading	3	95.20	95.60	94.70	93.80	93.60	93.30	92.00	91.20	
		5	94.30	93.60	94.20	91.70	91.10	90.40	89.00	89.00	
		7	95.30	94.80	95.50	93.90	93.60	92.50	92.70	92.10	70.40
		9	94.30	93.50	94.00	92.20	92.20	91.20	89.80	89.90	
	Spelling	3	94.50	94.90	92.70	92.20	90.50	90.50	88.80	90.50	62.60
		5	94.55	94.60	92.40	92.40	91.20	90.40	89.90	90.30	
		7	93.60	94.60	93.10	92.90	92.40	89.90	91.90	90.20	67.90
		9	90.90	91.60	91.10	89.70	89.30	86.80	88.20	87.50	
	Writing	3	96.30	97.15	95.90	95.60	95.20	96.60	93.60	95.10	74.40
		5	94.80	94.90	93.70	92.80	92.00	91.60	89.80	91.70	
		7	93.70	93.70	93.20	92.50	92.70	88.60	91.10	91.30	66.35
		9	90.30	89.00	89.60	87.70	87.80	83.60	85.00	86.20	
	Gramm...	3	95.60	94.90	94.30	92.50	92.20	91.30	89.40	88.50	
		5	94.90	93.70	94.40	92.00	91.30	89.90	89.60	88.90	
		7	94.20	92.50	94.30	92.00	92.20	90.10	90.80	89.60	61.55
		9	92.70	91.00	92.80	90.30	90.70	88.70	88.60	88.10	

GradeLevel
  ▾ 4 of 4 values
Domain
  ▾ 5 of 5 values
State
  ▾ 9 of 9 values
TestYear
  ⫶ 1 of 2 values

Figure 20—Heat matrix showing educational performance of Australian students by state/territory (http://tessera.com.au)

complexity and size based on the class or directory structure, which is what Panopticode does. Tree maps are most effective when the user can interact with them by drilling into and hovering over the rectangle representing the nominal data (for example, class/file/directory).

• *Bullet graphs*: Shown in Figure 22, *Bullet graph*, on page 214, a bullet graph is an alternative to speedometer gauges used in dashboards to visualize quantitative part-to-whole relationships, such as KPIs. Taking the example of a KPI, a bullet graph encodes the part and whole with lengths of varying hue and varying-intensity lengths in the background for ordinal measures of performance such as good, satisfactory, and bad. The closest real-life analogy would be a thermometer.

Exploring Connections and Networks

If you think about it, hierarchies and part-to-whole relationships express a specific type of connection between two or more things. For visualizing arbitrary interconnected relationships (including hierarchies and part-to-whole relationships), network graphs are a great option.

• *Network graphs*: These allow us to see connections, usually between nominal data, as a set of lines connecting nodes. Aside from the obvious options of encoding the nodes and lines, there are lots of ways to lay out the graph. Circular graphs aim to visualize a flat list of relationships. Hierarchical graphs use a treelike layout. Multilevel force-directed graphs use some physics and spring heuristics to space out the nodes in the

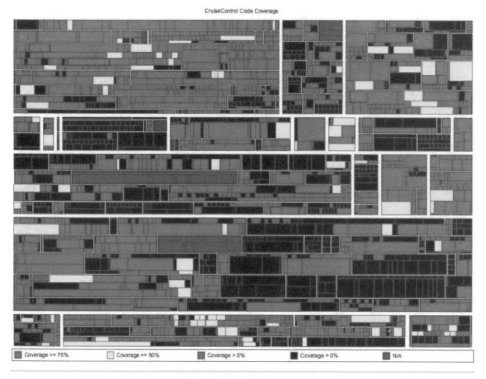

Figure 21—Tree map

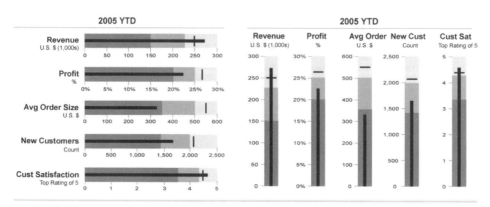

Figure 22—Bullet graph

graph. There are others, too, but the choice really depends on the nature of the data and the task at hand.

- *Edge bundling*: This is a technique that gives more clarity to network graphs by visually bundling adjacent edges together instead of using the shortest linear path between two nodes, thus resembling a well-organized layout of network cables in a server room (Figure 23, *Edge bundling (Danny Holten 2006)*, on page 215). The effectiveness of this approach is clearly evident when you notice the increased line widths and color intensity of bundled connections in a graph.

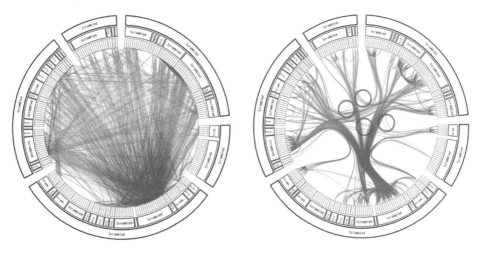

Figure 23—Edge bundling (Danny Holten 2006)

There are many other useful patterns in the wild. For example, you'll find heat maps commonly used in the financial services industry to view the activity of the stock market in real time, as shown in Figure 24, *Heat map showing changes in NASDAQ stocks on a given day*, on page 216. Keep an eye out for these patterns. Knowing their objectives and deconstructing the encodings and how they work will help you tailor/modify them for your own purpose. For the patterns I mentioned, you'll find many tools and frameworks out there to help you quickly implement them.

12.5 Tools and Frameworks

It's becoming increasingly important, and easy, for us to implement our own custom visualizations and the more common patterns described earlier. I believe that the ease with which people can implement their own visualizations will play a key role in the adoption of good visualization design practices.

Visualization Libraries

Browsers are getting better at accommodating visually heavy interfaces, and the tools for making such interfaces are evolving in step. The things you can

Figure 24—Heat map showing changes in NASDAQ stocks on a given day

do with HTML5 canvas and JavaScript were once a perk that only Flash and Java applets enjoyed, but now the landscape is changing. Some of those libraries are listed here. The best way to learn about your options is by visiting their websites, all of which have demo "galleries" and sample code.

- *Protovis*: Led by members of the Stanford Visualization Group, this is a popular open source JavaScript graphics library. In addition to providing a custom visualization API with animation support, it allows you to implement many common customizable visualizations, including all of those mentioned earlier. Protovis gives you a declarative, data-driven fluent API and is well grounded in good infovis practices and patterns.

- *Processing*: This is a mature open source programming language for infovis built on top of Java. It was first designed to produce Java applets but has now been ported for several other languages and platforms including JavaScript (Processing.js) and Flash/ActionScript (Processing.as).

- *Raphaël*: This is a promising open source JavaScript library that uses the SVG WC3 Recommendation and VML for creating graphics. As with Protovis, it has all the standard browser-based functionality and mechanisms for implementing client-side interfaces, such as DOM manipulation and events. GitHub uses Raphaël to visualize some metrics about its source code repositories. Raphaël also comes with animation support.

- *Standard charting libraries*: There are a multitude of charting and graphing libraries out there. These libraries aren't as flexible as the ones mentioned earlier since they focus more on providing functionality around standard precanned visualizations. Examples include Google Charts (image and Flash-based), Fusion Charts, flot (jQuery), and JavaScript InfoVis Toolkit.

Graphical Tools

When it comes to graphical tools, my observation is that there aren't as many generic infovis tools as there are more pattern-driven tools that let you create very specific visualizations. So, you obviously don't get as much flexibility here as you do with the infovis libraries discussed earlier. My experience with and knowledge of graphical tools is quite limited, so I can only recommend the following:

- *Tableau*: This is a flexible and generic visualization tool that is well aligned with the infovis design process discussed earlier. Measures, or data values of any type, can be visually encoded with a set of supported encodings, such as color, length, and area. Tableau also has good support for the data side of BI.

- *Panopticon*: This lets you create many of the visualizations discussed earlier and also comes with a developer SDK. In fact, the horizon graph was first introduced by Panopticon. The tool supports the creation of heat maps, heat matrices, time-series graphs, bullet graphs, and many more.

- *Many Eyes*: Although not a tool I'd rely on for mission-critical work, this is good for dipping your toes into infovis. Created by IBM, it is intended to be a social application for creating and sharing visualizations from uploaded data.

- *GraphViz*: This is a text-based tool that allows you to create network graphs using their simple DOT language by declaratively defining nodes and connections between them.

The landscape of tools and frameworks is evolving fairly quickly and will easily date this chapter. Whatever tool or framework you use, try your best to stick to the basic concepts and avoid getting distracted by seemingly cool features that add unnecessary bells and whistles. I often find myself stripping away many default properties just so I can build the simplest visualization that works.

12.6 Wrapping Up

Infovis is a broad and reemerging field, and we've only scratched the surface in this essay. Nonetheless, I hope you got a feel for the depth of this topic and the significant value it can bring to today's projects and organizations.

If you're the kind who tends to avoid visual design, remember that there is an objective side to design as well, as outlined in this essay. You don't need to be a Monet to be effective with and opinionated about visual communication. What you do need is to educate yourself on the objective facets of design and develop an appreciation for the subjective facets. For starters, I highly recommend reading books and articles by Stephen Few, Edware Tufte, and Colin Ware. Find a recurring analytical task that involves sifting through boring or multivariate data and give the visualization design process a shot.

The twenty-first century will continue to see unprecedented growth in information, especially as we find better ways of connecting disparate information. We're seeing it already with more blogs than we can follow, more articles than we can digest, more trends than we can keep up with, and more emerging markets than we can tap.

So, whether you're trying to understand your customers, make better-informed decisions for your organization, or convey a message to society, remember that you're really just capturing and presenting the information around you. You're trying to tell a story. In light of this fundamental premise of communication, try not to forget how much a picture is really worth.

Bibliography

[Arm07]   Joe Armstrong. *Programming Erlang: Software for a Concurrent World*. The Pragmatic Bookshelf, Raleigh, NC and Dallas, TX, 2007.

[BA04]   Kent Beck and Cynthia Andres. *Extreme Programming Explained: Embrace Change*. Addison-Wesley, Reading, MA, Second, 2004.

[Bec00]   Kent Beck. *Extreme Programming Explained: Embrace Change*. Addison-Wesley Longman, Reading, MA, 2000.

[Bec02]   Kent Beck. *Test Driven Development: By Example*. Addison-Wesley, Reading, MA, 2002.

[Bur11]   Trevor Burnham. *CoffeeScript: Accelerated JavaScript Development*. The Pragmatic Bookshelf, Raleigh, NC and Dallas, TX, 2011.

[CM08]   Wendy Chisholm and Matt May. *Universal Design for Web Applications*. O'Reilly & Associates, Inc., Sebastopol, CA, 2008.

[CT09]   Francesco Cesarini and Simon Thompson. *Erlang Programming*. O'Reilly & Associates, Inc., Sebastopol, CA, 2009.

[Coh04]   Mike Cohn. *User Stories Applied: For Agile Software Development*. Addison-Wesley Professional, Boston, MA, 2004.

[DMG07]   Paul Duvall, Steve Matyas, and Andrew Glover. *Continuous Integration: Improving Software Quality and Reducing Risk*. Addison-Wesley, Reading, MA, 2007.

[FBBO99]   Martin Fowler, Kent Beck, John Brant, William Opdyke, and Don Roberts. *Refactoring: Improving the Design of Existing Code*. Addison-Wesley, Reading, MA, 1999.

[FH11]   Michael Fogus and Chris Houser. *The Joy of Clojure*. Manning Publications Co., Greenwich, CT, 2011.

[FPMW04] Steve Freeman, Nat Pryce, Tim Mackinnon, and Joe Walnes. Mock Roles, Not Objects. *OOPSLA '04: Companion to the 19th annual ACM SIGPLAN conference on Object-oriented programming systems, languages, and applications.* :236–246, 2004.

[Few06]   Stephen Few. *Information Dashboard Design: The Effective Visual Communication of Data.* O'Reilly & Associates, Inc., Sebastopol, CA, 2006.

[GHJV95] Erich Gamma, Richard Helm, Ralph Johnson, and John Vlissides. *Design Patterns: Elements of Reusable Object-Oriented Software.* Addison-Wesley, Reading, MA, 1995.

[Gau02]   Hugh G. Gauch Jr. *Scientific Method in Practice.* Cambridge University Press, Cambridge, United Kingdom, 2002.

[Gra10]   Dave Gray. *Gamestorming: A Playbook for Innovators, Rulebreakers, and Changemakers.* O'Reilly & Associates, Inc., Sebastopol, CA, 2010.

[HF10]   Jez Humble and David Farley. *Continuous Delivery: Reliable Software Releases Through Build, Test, and Deployment Automation.* Addison-Wesley, Reading, MA, 2010.

[Hal09]   Stuart Halloway. *Programming Clojure.* The Pragmatic Bookshelf, Raleigh, NC and Dallas, TX, 2009.

[Hoh06]   Luke Hohmann. *Innovation Games: Creating Breakthrough Products Through Collaborative Play.* Addison-Wesley Longman, Reading, MA, 2006.

[Inc08]   ThoughtWorks Inc. *ThoughtWorks Anthology.* The Pragmatic Bookshelf, Raleigh, NC and Dallas, TX, 2008.

[Mol09]   Ian Molyneaux. *The Art of Application Performance Testing.* O'Reilly & Associates, Inc., Sebastopol, CA, 2009.

[Nyg07]   Michael T. Nygard. *Release It!: Design and Deploy Production-Ready Software.* The Pragmatic Bookshelf, Raleigh, NC and Dallas, TX, 2007.

[OGS08]   Bryan O'Sullivan, John Goerzen, and Donald Bruce Stewart. *Real World Haskell.* O'Reilly & Associates, Inc., Sebastopol, CA, 2008.

[OSV08]   Martin Odersky, Lex Spoon, and Bill Venners. *Programming in Scala.* Artima, Inc., Mountain View, CA, Second, 2008.

[RWL95]   Trygve Reenskaug, Per Wold, and Odd Arild Lehne. *Working With Objects: The OOram Software Engineering Method.* Prentice Hall, Englewood Cliffs, NJ, 1995.

[War08]   Colin Ware. *Visual Thinking: for Design.* Morgan Kaufmann Publishers, San Francisco, CA, 2008.

Index

Career++

Ready to kick your career up to the next level? Start by growing a significant online presence, and then reinvigorate your job itself.

Technical Blogging is the first book to specifically teach programmers, technical people, and technically-oriented entrepreneurs how to become successful bloggers. There is no magic to successful blogging; with this book you'll learn the techniques to attract and keep a large audience of loyal, regular readers and leverage this popularity to achieve your goals.

Antonio Cangiano
(304 pages) ISBN: 9781934356883. $33
http://pragprog.com/titles/actb

You're already a great coder, but awesome coding chops aren't always enough to get you through your toughest projects. You need these 50+ nuggets of wisdom. Veteran programmers: reinvigorate your passion for developing web applications. New programmers: here's the guidance you need to get started. With this book, you'll think about your job in new and enlightened ways.

Ka Wai Cheung
(250 pages) ISBN: 9781934356791. $29
http://pragprog.com/titles/kcdc